Excel 2013:
Advanced
Student Manual

Excel 2013: Advanced

Chief Executive Officer, Axzo Press:	Ken Wasnock
Series Designer and COO:	Adam A. Wilcox
Vice President, Operations:	Josh Pincus
Director of Publishing Systems Development:	Dan Quackenbush
Writer:	Micky Markert
Keytester:	Cliff Coryea

Trademarks

ILT Series is a trademark of Axzo Press.

Some of the product names and company names used in this book have been used for identification purposes only and may be trademarks or registered trademarks of their respective manufacturers and sellers.

Disclaimer

We reserve the right to revise this publication and make changes from time to time in its content without notice.

ISBN 10: 1-4260-3610-8
ISBN 13: 978-1-4260-3610-1

Printed in the United States of America

1 2 3 4 5 GL 06 05 04 03

Contents

Introduction

After reading this introduction, you will know how to:

A Use ILT Series manuals in general.

B Use prerequisites, a target student description, course objectives, and a skills inventory to properly set your expectations for the course.

C Re-key this course after class.

Topic A: About the manual

ILT Series philosophy

Our manuals facilitate your learning by providing structured interaction with the software itself. While we provide text to explain difficult concepts, the hands-on activities are the focus of our courses. By paying close attention as your instructor leads you through these activities, you will learn the skills and concepts effectively.

We believe strongly in the instructor-led class. During class, focus on your instructor. Our manuals are designed and written to facilitate your interaction with your instructor, and not to call attention to manuals themselves.

We believe in the basic approach of setting expectations, delivering instruction, and providing summary and review afterwards. For this reason, lessons begin with objectives and end with summaries. We also provide overall course objectives and a course summary to provide both an introduction to and closure on the entire course.

Manual components

The manuals contain these major components:

- Table of contents
- Introduction
- Units
- Course summary
- Glossary
- Index

Each element is described below.

Table of contents

The table of contents acts as a learning roadmap.

Introduction

The introduction contains information about our training philosophy and our manual components, features, and conventions. It contains target student, prerequisite, objective, and setup information for the specific course.

Units

Units are the largest structural component of the course content. A unit begins with a title page that lists objectives for each major subdivision, or topic, within the unit. Within each topic, conceptual and explanatory information alternates with hands-on activities. Units conclude with a summary comprising one paragraph for each topic, and an independent practice activity that gives you an opportunity to practice the skills you've learned.

The conceptual information takes the form of text paragraphs, exhibits, lists, and tables. The activities are structured in two columns, one telling you what to do, the other providing explanations, descriptions, and graphics.

Course summary

This section provides a text summary of the entire course. It is useful for providing closure at the end of the course. The course summary also indicates the next course in this series, if there is one, and lists additional resources you might find useful as you continue to learn about the software.

Glossary

The glossary provides definitions for all of the key terms used in this course.

Index

The index at the end of this manual makes it easy for you to find information about a particular software component, feature, or concept.

Manual conventions

We've tried to keep the number of elements and the types of formatting to a minimum in the manuals. This aids in clarity and makes the manuals more classically elegant looking. But there are some conventions and icons you should know about.

Item	Description
Italic text	In conceptual text, indicates a new term or feature.
Bold text	In unit summaries, indicates a key term or concept. In an independent practice activity, indicates an explicit item that you select, choose, or type.
`Code font`	Indicates code or syntax.
`Longer strings of ▶ code will look ▶ like this.`	In the hands-on activities, any code that's too long to fit on a single line is divided into segments by one or more continuation characters (▶). This code should be entered as a continuous string of text.
Select **bold item**	In the left column of hands-on activities, bold sans-serif text indicates an explicit item that you select, choose, or type.
Keycaps like (↵ ENTER)	Indicate a key on the keyboard you must press.

Hands-on activities

The hands-on activities are the most important parts of our manuals. They are divided into two primary columns. The "Here's how" column gives short instructions to you about what to do. The "Here's why" column provides explanations, graphics, and clarifications. Here's a sample:

Do it!

A-1:   Creating a commission formula

Here's how	Here's why
1 Open Sales	This is an oversimplified sales compensation worksheet. It shows sales totals, commissions, and incentives for five sales reps.
2 Observe the contents of cell F4	`F4` ▾ = `=E4*C_Rate` The commission rate formulas use the name "C_Rate" instead of a value for the commission rate.

For these activities, we have provided a collection of data files designed to help you learn each skill in a real-world business context. As you work through the activities, you will modify and update these files. Of course, you might make a mistake and therefore want to re-key the activity starting from scratch. To make it easy to start over, you will rename each data file at the end of the first activity in which the file is modified. Our convention for renaming files is to add the word "My" to the beginning of the file name. In the above activity, for example, a file called "Sales" is being used for the first time. At the end of this activity, you would save the file as "My sales," thus leaving the "Sales" file unchanged. If you make a mistake, you can start over using the original "Sales" file.

In some activities, however, it might not be practical to rename the data file. If you want to retry one of these activities, ask your instructor for a fresh copy of the original data file.

Topic B: Setting your expectations

Properly setting your expectations is essential to your success. This topic will help you do that by providing:

- Prerequisites for this course
- A description of the target student
- A list of the objectives for the course
- A skills assessment for the course

Course prerequisites

Before taking this course, you should be familiar with personal computers and the use of a keyboard and a mouse. Furthermore, this course assumes that you've completed the following courses or have equivalent experience:

- *Windows 7: Basic, Windows Vista: Basic,* or *Windows XP: Basic*
- *Excel 2013: Basic*
- *Excel 2013: Intermediate*

Target student

Before taking this course, you should be comfortable using a personal computer and Microsoft Windows (preferably, Windows 7). You should have some experience with Excel 2013 and should be familiar with intermediate-level tasks, such as sorting data, linking worksheets, and outlining and consolidating data. You will get the most out of this course if their goal is to become proficient in performing advanced tasks, such as using logical, statistical, financial, and date functions, working with data tables, validating cell entries and using advanced filters, creating advanced charts, working with PivotTables and PivotCharts, exporting and importing data, performing what-if analyses, and recording macros.

Course objectives

These overall course objectives will give you an idea about what to expect from the course. It is also possible that they will help you see that this course is not the right one for you. If you think you either lack the prerequisite knowledge or already know most of the subject matter to be covered, you should let your instructor know that you think you are misplaced in the class.

After completing this course, you will know how to:

- Use the IF and IFERROR functions to calculate a value based on specified criteria; use conditional functions to summarize data; use the PMT function to calculate periodic payments for a loan; use text functions to extract data strings; use date functions to calculate duration in years, months, and days; create array formulas to perform multiple calculations on multiple sets of data at one time; and change calculation options and iteration limits.

- Use the VLOOKUP and HLOOKUP functions to find values in worksheet data; use the MATCH function to find the relative position of a value in a range; use the INDEX function to find the value of a cell at a given position in a range; and use data tables to project values.

- Use the Data Validation feature to validate data entered in cells; and use advanced filter options to display the data you specify.

- Format data points in charts; create combination charts and trendlines; insert sparklines; use chart templates; and add and modify drawing objects and shapes.

- Create a PivotTable for analyzing and comparing large amounts of data; modify the PivotTable view by using slicers to filter data and by rearranging fields; improve the appearance of a PivotTable by changing its field settings and applying a style; and create a PivotChart to graphically display data from a PivotTable.

- Export data from Excel to other formats, and import data from a text file into an Excel workbook; and use Microsoft Query and the Web query feature to import data from external databases.

- Use the Goal Seek utility to meet a target output for a formula by adjusting the values in the input cells; and create scenarios to save various sets of input values that produce different results.

- Run a macro to perform tasks automatically; record macros; assign a macro to a button in the worksheet; edit a macro by editing VBA code.

Skills inventory

Use the following form to gauge your skill level entering the class. For each skill listed, rate your familiarity from 1 to 5, with five being the most familiar. *This is not a test.* Rather, it is intended to provide you with an idea of where you're starting from at the beginning of class. If you're wholly unfamiliar with all the skills, you might not be ready for the class. If you think you already understand all of the skills, you might need to move on to the next course in the series. In either case, you should let your instructor know as soon as possible.

Skill	1	2	3	4	5
Using logical functions (IF, IFERROR)					
Using a formula to apply conditional formatting					
Using math and statistical functions (SUMIF, COUNTIF, AVERAGEIF, SUMIFS, COUNTIFS, AVERAGEIFS, ROUND)					
Using the PMT function					
Using text functions (LEFT, RIGHT, MID, LEN, FIND)					
Using date functions (TODAY, DAYS360, and NETWORKDAYS)					
Creating array formulas					
Using the VLOOKUP, MATCH, and INDEX functions					
Using data tables to project values					
Validating data					
Using advanced filtering options					
Adjusting the scale of a chart and formatting data points					
Creating combination charts and trendlines					
Inserting sparklines					
Creating a custom chart template					
Adding and formatting graphics in a chart					
Creating, rearranging, and formatting PivotTables					
Using slicers to filter PivotTable data					
Creating PivotCharts					
Importing and exporting text files					

Skill	1	2	3	4	5
Using Microsoft Query and Web query					
Using Goal Seek					
Creating scenarios					
Running and recording macros					
Assigning macros to buttons					
Editing VBA modules					

Topic C: Re-keying the course

If you have the proper hardware and software, you can re-key this course after class. This section explains what you'll need in order to do so, and how to do it.

Hardware requirements

Your personal computer should have:

- 1 GHz or faster 32- or 64-bit processor
- At least 1 GB of RAM
- 2 GB of hard-disk space after operating system install
- Video adapter card compatible with DirectX 9 or newer, with at least 64 MB video memory
- A keyboard and a mouse
- A monitor with at least 1024 × 768 resolution
- Printer (useful but not required)
- DVD drive if you'll be installing via disc

Software requirements

You will also need the following software:

- Windows 7 Professional or Ultimate. (You can also use Windows XP or Windows Vista, but the screen shots in this course were taken in Windows 7, so your screens might look somewhat different.)
- Microsoft Office Professional Plus 2013
- A printer driver (An actual printer is not required, but you will not be able to get an exact preview in Print Preview without a printer driver installed.)

Network requirements

The following network components and connectivity are also required for re-keying this course:

- Internet access, for the following purposes:
    - Updating the Windows operating system and Microsoft Office 2013

Setup instructions to re-key the course

Before you re-key the course, you will need to perform the following steps.

1   Use Windows Update to install all available critical updates and service packs.

2   With a flat-panel display, we recommend using the panel's native resolution for best results. Color depth/quality should be set to High (24 bit) or higher.

   Please note that your display settings or resolution may differ from the author's, so your screens might not exactly match the screen shots in this manual.

3   If necessary, reset any Excel 2013 defaults that you have changed. If you do not wish to reset the defaults, you can still re-key the course, but some activities might not work exactly as documented.

   • In the Excel Options dialog box, reset the Quick Access Toolbar to its default state.

4   If you have the data disc that came with this manual, locate the Student Data folder on it and copy it to your Windows desktop.

   If you don't have the data disc, you can download the Student Data files for the course:

   a   Connect to http://downloads.logicaloperations.com.
   b   Enter the course title or search by part to locate this course
   c   Click the course title to display a list of available downloads.
       Note: Data Files are located under the Instructor Edition of the course.
   d   Click the link(s) for downloading the Student Data files.
   e   Create a folder named Student Data on the desktop of your computer.
   f   Double-click the downloaded zip file(s) and drag the contents into the Student Data folder.

Unit 1
Advanced functions and formulas

Complete this unit, and you'll know how to:

A Use logical functions to calculate values based on specified criteria.

B Use conditional functions to summarize, count, and average data.

C Use the PMT function to calculate periodic payments for a loan.

D Use text functions to extract specific text strings from cells.

E Use date functions to calculate duration, expressed as the number of days.

F Use array formulas to perform multiple calculations on multiple sets of values.

Topic A: Logical functions

Explanation

You can use conditional logic in a formula to return a specific result depending on whether a certain test, or condition, is met. If the condition is true, one result will be displayed. If the condition is false, a different result will be displayed. Microsoft Excel 2013 provides several logical functions you can use for conditionally evaluating a calculation. In this topic, we'll look at IF, and IFERROR.

The IF function

The IF function evaluates a condition, or logical test. If the condition is true, the function returns a specific value. Otherwise, it returns another value. The syntax of the IF function is:

```
IF(logical_test,value_if_true,value_if_false)
```

In this syntax, `logical_test` is the criterion you want the function to evaluate, `value_if_true` is the value to be returned if the condition is true, and `value_if_false` is the value to be returned if the condition is false.

Editing conditions in a formula

The techniques used to edit formulas are the same as those used to edit other cell data. You can either:

- Click the formula bar to edit the formula.
- Double-click the cell and edit the formula in the cell.

When the formula is activated, the color of the cell references in the formula match the outline color in the worksheet. Also, the ScreenTip identifies the function component that is being edited. In Exhibit 1-1, for example, the insertion point is in the middle of the logical test, so "logical_test" is bold.

	A	B	C	D	E	F	G	H	I
				Outlander Spices					
				Commission report					
	Sales goal:	$8,500							
	Salesperson	Sales per quarter				Total sales	Commission		
		Qtr1	Qtr2	Qtr3	Qtr4				
	Bill MacArthur	$2,500	$2,750	$3,500	$3,700		=IF(F8>$B$4,F8*2%,"NA")		
	Jamie Morrison	$3,560	$3,000	$1,700	$2,000	$10,260	IF(logical_test, [value_if_true], [value_if_false])		
	Maureen O'Connor	$4,500	$4,000	$3,500	$3,700	$15,700	$314		
	Rebecca Austin	$3,250	$2,725	$3,000	$3,250	$12,225	$245		
	Paul Anderson	$2,520	$2,000	$2,500	$2,700	$9,720	$194		
	Cynthia Roberts	$1,500	$1,700	$1,800	$2,000	$7,000	NA		
	Rita Greg	$4,590	$4,050	$4,500	$3,700	$16,840	$337		
	Trevor Johnson	$3,660	$3,200	$3,000	$2,250	$12,110	$242		
	Kevin Meyers	$1,790	$1,800	$2,000	$2,200	$7,790	NA		
	Adam Long	$1,700	$1,950	$2,500	$2,750	$8,900	$178		
	Kendra James	$1,650	$2,000	$1,500	$1,750	$6,900	NA		
	Michael Lee	$2,050	$2,500	$2,800	$3,200	$10,550	$211		
	Sandra Lawrence	$3,425	$3,750	$4,000	$3,120	$14,295	$286		
	Mary Smith	$4,540	$2,700	$3,000	$3,200	$13,440	$269		
	Annie Philips	$1,200	$1,700	$1,800	$2,000	$6,700	NA		

Exhibit 1-1: Editing a formula

Do it!

A-1: Using the IF function

The files for this activity are in Student Data folder **Unit 1\Topic A**.

Here's how	Here's why
1 Start Excel 2013	
2 Open Commission.xlsx	In the current topic folder.
3 Save the workbook as **My Commission.xlsx**	
4 Select G8	If necessary. You'll use the IF function to calculate the commission for each salesperson. If the total-sales value is greater than the sales-goal value in cell B4, the commission should be calculated as 2% of the total sales. Otherwise, "NA" should appear in the cell.
Type **=IF(F8>$B$4,**	In this function, "F8>$B$4" is the condition that will be evaluated. The reference to B4 is absolute (expressed as $B$4) because you'll AutoFill the cell to the ones below, and the other formulas should all refer to B4.
5 Type **F8*2%,**	"F8*2%" is the value to be returned if the condition is true.
Type **"NA")**	"NA" is the value to be returned if the condition is false.

6 Press [↵ ENTER]	The value NA appears in G8. Because the condition F8>B4 is false ($7,450<$8,500), the value NA is returned.
7 Copy the formula in G8 to G9:G22	(Use the AutoFill handle.) To calculate the remaining commissions.
Observe the Commission column	

Commission
NA
$205
$314
$245
$194
NA
$337
$242
NA
$178
NA
$211
$286
$269
NA

You'll see the commission amount for each salesperson.

8 Double-click G8	To edit the formula directly in the cell. Notice that the B4 cell reference in the formula and the cell outline are the same red color. This color coding can be useful when you're editing complicated formulas.
Press [ESC]	To close Edit mode.
9 Update the workbook	

The IFERROR function

Explanation

You can use the IFERROR function to check a formula for errors and to replace Excel's default error message with a message you specify. For example, if you try to divide a number by zero in a formula, the error message #DIV/0! appears in the cell by default. You can replace this message with your own by using IFERROR.

The syntax for the IFERROR function is:

```
IFERROR(value,value_if_error)
```

where `value` is the argument you want to check for an error, and `value_if_error` is the message you want to display if an error is found. If no error is found in the formula, the result of the formula is displayed.

Do it!

A-2:   Using the IFERROR function

Here's how	Here's why
1 Click the IFERROR sheet	You'll use the IFERROR function to find calculation errors and identify them with your own error message.
2 Select D7	
Type **=IFERROR(**	To begin the IFERROR function.
Type **B7/C7,**	To enter the value you want the function to calculate and check for errors.
3 Type **"Check price")**	To specify the error message to be displayed if the function finds an error.
Press ↵ ENTER	To complete the formula and calculate a result for D7.
4 Copy the formula in D7 to D8:D19	The error message "Check price" appears in D8 and D18 because the formula tried to divide a number by zero.
5 Update and close the workbook	

Topic B: Conditional functions

The SUMIF function

Explanation

You can conditionally summarize, count, and average data by using math and statistical functions. These functions include SUMIF, COUNTIF, AVERAGEIF, SUMIFS, COUNTIFS, and AVERAGEIFS.

You use the SUMIF function when you want to add values within a range of cells based on the evaluation of a criterion in another range. The syntax of the SUMIF function is:

```
SUMIF(range,criteria,sum_range)
```

In this syntax, `range` is the range in which the function will test the criterion specified in `criteria`. The argument `sum_range` specifies the actual cells whose values are to be added. `Sum_range` is optional; if it's omitted, the cells specified in `range` are evaluated by `criteria`, and they are added if they match `criteria`.

Summary					
East			**North**		
Total sales-prior year	$43,685.00		Total sales-prior year		$65,040.00
Total sales-current year	$56,320.00		Total sales-current year		$70,950.00
Current year average			Current year average		
Increase above target			Increase above target		
Stores over target			Stores over target		
Average increase			Average increase		
South			**West**		
Total sales-prior year	$35,465.00		Total sales-prior year		$28,600.00
Total sales-current year	$44,680.00		Total sales-current year		$39,980.00
Current year average			Current year average		
Increase above target			Increase above target		
Stores over target			Stores over target		
Average increase			Average increase		

Exhibit 1-2: The SUMIF function applied

Do it!

B-1:   Using SUMIF

The files for this activity are in Student Data folder **Unit 1\Topic B**.

Here's how	Here's why
1 Open Sales.xlsx	In the current topic folder.
Save the workbook as **My Sales.xlsx**	
2 Select B29	You'll sum up the sales for the East region for the prior year.
Type **=SUMIF(Region,**	In the formula, "Region" is the named range of cells B8:B22, which SUMIF will evaluate.
Type **"East",**	"East" is the evaluation criterion. You must include quotes around this value because it is a label.
3 Type **Sales_prior)**	"Sales_prior" is the range C8:C22, which will be summed based on the criterion.
Press (↵ ENTER)	The value of the East region's total sales for the prior year, $43,685.00, appears in B29.
4 In B30, display the East region's total sales for the current year	(Use the name of the range D8:D22, Sales_current, in the SUMIF function.) The value $56,320.00 appears.
5 In E29, display the North region's total sales for the prior year	(Specify North as the evaluation criterion.) The value $65,040.00 appears.
6 In E30, display the North region's total sales for the current year	The value $70,950.00 appears.
7 Fill in the current and prior years' sales information for the South and West regions	Compare your results to Exhibit 1-2.
8 Update the workbook	

The COUNTIF function

Explanation

You use the COUNTIF function to count the number of cells in a range that meet your specified criteria.

The syntax for the COUNTIF function is:

`COUNTIF(range,criteria)`

`Range` is the cell or range of cells to count that meet the stated criterion. Text values and blank cells are ignored. `Criteria` can be text, numbers, expressions, or cell references that identify the cells to be counted.

Do it!

B-2:   Using COUNTIF

Here's how	Here's why
1 Select G8	You'll count the number of stores that have met or exceeded the current year's sales goal of $15,000.
2 Type **=COUNTIF(**	To start the function.
Type **Sales_current,**	To designate the range in which you will count the cells that meet your criterion.
Type **">=15000")**	To specify the criterion to be met.
3 Press (← ENTER)	To complete the function and return the result. The value 9 appears in the cell because there are nine stores meeting or exceeding the sales goal.
4 Update the workbook	

The AVERAGEIF function

Explanation

AVERAGEIF, like SUMIF and COUNTIF, is a conditional math function. Use AVERAGEIF to conditionally average a range of numbers.

The syntax for the AVERAGEIF function is:

`AVERAGEIF(range,criteria,average_range)`

`Range` is the cell or range of cells you want to average, and `criteria` is the number, expression, cell reference, or text that identifies which cells should be averaged. `Average_range` is the corresponding set of cells you want to average. If you omit this, `range` will be used instead.

Summary					
East			**North**		
Total sales-prior year	$43,685.00		Total sales-prior year	$65,040.00	
Total sales-current year	$56,320.00		Total sales-current year	$70,950.00	
Current year average	$14,080.00		Current year average	$17,737.50	
Increase above target			Increase above target		
Stores over target			Stores over target		
Average increase			Average increase		
South			**West**		
Total sales-prior year	$35,465.00		Total sales-prior year	$28,600.00	
Total sales-current year	$44,680.00		Total sales-current year	$39,980.00	
Current year average	$11,170.00		Current year average	$13,326.67	
Increase above target			Increase above target		
Stores over target			Stores over target		
Average increase			Average increase		

Exhibit 1-3: The AVERAGEIF function applied

Do it!

B-3: Using AVERAGEIF

Here's how	Here's why
1 Select B31	You'll calculate the average of current-year sales for the East region.
2 Type **=AVERAGEIF(**	To begin the function.
Type **Region,"East",**	To designate Region as the range, and East as the criterion for that range.
Type **Sales_current)**	To designate the current year's sales in column D as the range from which the actual cells to be averaged will be drawn.
3 Press ⏎ ENTER	To finish the function and calculate the result. Cell B31displays $14,080.00, which is the average of current-year sales for the East region.
4 Calculate the average of current-year sales for the remaining regions	Compare your results to Exhibit 1-3.
5 Update the workbook	

SUMIFS, COUNTIFS, and AVERAGEIFS

Explanation

Although SUMIF, COUNTIF, and AVERAGEIF are useful for conditionally summarizing data, they allow only one criterion. To remedy this limitation, Excel provides the SUMIFS, COUNTIFS, and AVERAGEIFS functions, which enable you to easily sum, count, and average values in a range while using multiple criteria.

SUMIFS

The syntax for the SUMIFS function is:

```
SUMIFS(sum_range,criteria_range1,criteria1,criteria_range2,
criteria2)
```

Sum_range is the cell or range you want to sum. Criteria_range1 and criteria_range2 are the ranges in which the function evaluates the related criteria; criteria1 and criteria2 are the actual criteria. Note that in the SUMIFS function, the sum_range argument appears first (rather than last, as in SUMIF).

COUNTIFS

The syntax for the COUNTIFS function is:

```
COUNTIFS(range1,criteria1,range2,criteria2)
```

Range1 and range2 are the ranges where the related criteria are evaluated. Criteria1 and criteria2 are the criteria by which the cells or ranges are evaluated.

AVERAGEIFS

The syntax for the AVERAGEIFS function is:

```
AVERAGEIFS(average_range,criteria_range1,criteria1,
criteria_range2,criteria2)
```

Average_range is the range of cells you want to average. Criteria_range1 and criteria_range2 are the ranges where the function evaluates the related criteria. Criteria1 and criteria2 are the criteria by which the specified cells will be evaluated.

Summary				
East			**North**	
Total sales-prior year	$43,685.00		Total sales-prior year	$65,040.00
Total sales-current year	$56,320.00		Total sales-current year	$70,950.00
Current year average	$14,080.00		Current year average	$17,737.50
Increase above target	$6,985.00		Increase above target	$3,660.00
Stores over target	2		Stores over target	3
Average increase	$3,492.50		Average increase	$1,220.00
South			**West**	
Total sales-prior year	$35,465.00		Total sales-prior year	$28,600.00
Total sales-current year	$44,680.00		Total sales-current year	$39,980.00
Current year average	$11,170.00		Current year average	$13,326.67
Increase above target	$7,105.00		Increase above target	$5,630.00
Stores over target	2		Stores over target	1
Average increase	$3,552.50		Average increase	$5,630.00

Exhibit 1-4: The completed Summary section

Do it!

B-4: Using SUMIFS, COUNTIFS, and AVERAGEIFS

Here's how	Here's why
1 Select B32	You'll use the SUMIFS function to sum the increase in sales over the target goal for stores in the East region.
2 Type =**SUMIFS(**	To begin the function.
Type **E8:E22,**	To specify the range containing the cells to be summarized. You want to use the amount of increase or decrease in sales.
Type **Region,"East",**	To specify the East region as the first criteria range and the first criterion by which to evaluate the range.
Type **Sales_current,">15000")**	To specify the second criteria range and the second criterion. The formula will check to see if the current sales number is larger than the target of $15,000.
3 Press (↵ ENTER)	To enter the function. The value $6,985.00 is displayed. This is the total of the increase in sales over the target goal for all stores in the East region.
4 Calculate the increase in sales above the target goal for the remaining regions	Compare your results to the relevant cells in Exhibit 1-4.

5 Select B33	You'll calculate the number of stores in the East region that exceeded the target sales goal.
Type **=COUNTIFS(**	To begin the function.
6 Type **Region,"East",**	To specify the first range and the criterion by which the range will be evaluated.
Type **Sales_current,">15000")**	To specify the second range and the criterion by which it will be evaluated.
7 Press ⏎ ENTER	To complete the function and display the result. Two stores in the East region exceeded the sales target of $15,000.
Calculate the number of stores exceeding the target sales goal in each of the remaining regions	Compare your results to the relevant cells in Exhibit 1-4.
8 Select B34	You'll use the AVERAGEIFS function to calculate the average increase in sales for those stores exceeding the target goal.
9 Type **=AVERAGEIFS(**	To begin the function.
Type **E8:E22,**	To specify the range containing the cells to be averaged.
Type **Region,"East",**	To specify the first criteria range and the first criterion.
10 Type **Sales_current,">15000")**	To specify the second criteria range and the second criterion.
Press ⏎ ENTER	To complete the function and display the result; $3,492.50 appears in B34.
11 Calculate the average increase in sales for the remaining regions	Compare your Summary section to Exhibit 1-4.
Update and close the workbook	

Topic C: Financial functions

The PMT function

Explanation

Excel provides several financial functions for calculating such values as depreciation, future or present loan values, and loan payments. One financial function is the PMT function, which you can use to calculate loan payments.

The PMT function returns the periodic payments for a loan. The return value is negative if the amount is to be paid, and positive if the amount is to be obtained.

The syntax of the PMT function is:

    PMT(rate,nper,pv,fv,type)

The following table describes each argument of the PMT function:

Argument	Description
rate	The interest rate per period. For example, if you get a loan at 10% annual interest and you make monthly payments, the first argument will be 10%/12.
nper	The number of payments that have to be made to repay the loan. For example, if you have four years to pay back the loan, and you make monthly payments, the second argument will be 48 (4*12).
pv	The present value or the principal amount of the loan. This argument can also have a negative value. For example, if you give a loan of $12,000, the present value will be -12000. However, if you take a loan of $12,000, the present value will be 12000.
fv	(Optional) The future value of the loan—that is, its value after the last payment is made. If you omit the future value, it's assumed to be zero.
type	(Optional) Indicates when payments are due. This argument can have either of two values: 0 if payments are due at the end of the period, or 1 if payments are due at the beginning of the period. If you omit this argument, it's assumed to be zero.

Do it!   **C-1:   Using the PMT function**

The files for this activity are in Student Data folder **Unit 1\Topic C**.

Here's how	Here's why
1 Open Loan.xlsx	In the current topic folder.
Save the workbook as **My Loan.xlsx**	
2 Select E6	You'll calculate the monthly payment to be made to AmericaBank.
Type **=PMT(D6%/12,**	In this formula, "D6%/12" is the monthly rate of interest.
Type **C6,B6)**	`=PMT(D6%/12,C6,B6)`
	"C6" refers to the cell containing the period of repayment, and "B6" refers to the cell containing the present value of the loan.
Press (↵ ENTER)	The value -$3,417.76 appears in E6. The negative sign signifies that you have to pay this amount.
3 Copy the formula in E6 to E7:E8 and E10:E11	To calculate the monthly payments for the remaining banks.
4 Change the value in C6 to **24**	When the number of payments goes down, the monthly payment amount increases.
5 Update and close the workbook	

Topic D: **Text functions**

Splitting column data with text functions

You can use text functions to manipulate or modify strings of text. For example, you may want to split up a text string so that portions of it appear in separate columns. You can save hours of effort by using a text function to do the work for you.

Let's say you were sent a file with a column that includes both product numbers and product names. You want to be able to split that information into two separate columns. Rather than retype the data from scratch, use a text function to accomplish the task.

The LEFT and RIGHT functions

The LEFT text function will extract a specified number of characters from the leftmost portion of a text string, and return the result in the cell you designate. The syntax is:

```
=LEFT(text,[num_chars])
```

Text is the text, or cell reference, containing the string you want to manipulate, and num_chars is the number of characters you want the function to extract. So for example:

```
=LEFT (A3,7)
```

would extract 7 characters in the leftmost portion of the text string in cell A3.

As you might expect, the RIGHT function will perform similarly, only from the rightmost portion of the string:

```
=RIGHT(text,[num_chars])
```

The MID function

The MID function, as its name implies, will extract text from the middle of a string. It's a slightly more complicated function that LEFT or RIGHT, however, because it contains an additional argument:

```
=MID(text,start_num,num_chars)
```

Here, the start_num argument is the starting position of the first character of the text you want to extract. So for example:

```
=MID(A3,5,6)
```

would extract six characters from the string, beginning at the fifth position in the string. Keep in mind that characters can be letters, numbers, symbols, punctuation, and spaces.

Do it! **D-1: Using the LEFT, RIGHT, and MID functions**

The files for this activity are in Student Data folder **Unit 1\Topic D**.

Here's how	Here's why
1 Open Employee review.xlsx	In the current topic folder.
Save the workbook as **My Employee review.xlsx**	You've received a file containing employee information. The sender put different types of data into single columns, which makes the data hard to read, and less useful than it could be.
2 Observe column A	The text strings in this column look like meaningless numbers. However, they contain employee numbers, review information, and pay grades. You'll separate this information into three columns.
3 Activate C2	This column is where you'll extract the employee numbers, which are the four digits at the beginning of each text string in Column A.
4 Type **=LEFT(A2, 4)**	To extract the four leftmost characters from the text string in A2.
Press (↵ ENTER)	To return the result in C2. The Employee number is E001.
5 Fill the remaining employee number values in the C column	Use the AutoFill handle to copy the function.
6 Activate F2	This column will contain the employee pay grades, which are the last three digits of the text strings in column A.
Enter **=RIGHT(A2,3)**	To extract the three rightmost characters from the text string in A2.
Fill in the remaining pay grade values in column F	
7 Activate G2	You fill the review completion in this column. The review completion is in the middle of the text strings in column A.
Type **=MID(A2,5,1)**	The review completion value begin in the 5th character position of the text string, and is one character long.
Press (↵ ENTER)	To extract the review information in A2 to G2.
Fill in the remaining data values in column G	
8 Update the workbook	

The FIND and LEN functions

Explanation

The LEFT, RIGHT, and MID functions work well for extracting text strings that are a consistent length. However, you may find that you need to extract portions of a string that are not a uniform number of characters. In these cases you can use functions such as FIND and LEN.

You can use the FIND function to locate the position of a particular character or string within another string. The syntax for FIND is:

```
FIND(find_text,within_text,[start_num])
```

where `find_text` is the location of the text you want to find; `within_text` is the string that contains the text you want to find; and `start_num` specifies the character position at which you want to start the search.

`Start_num` is an optional argument. The first character in the `within_text` string is 1. If you don't use `start_num` in your formula, its value is assumed to be 1.

For example, say you have a phone number XXX-XXXX in A1, and you want to find the location of the – within it. You would enter

```
=FIND("-",A1)
```

to get the result of 4, since that is the position of the – character in the string.

The LEN function will return the number of characters of any string you specify. The syntax for LEN is:

```
LEN(text)
```

where `(text)` is the string or cell reference you want to find the length of.

For example, `=LEN(B2)` will return the number of characters in cell B2. Similarly, `=LEN("E015")` will return a result of 4, the number of characters in the string specified between the quotes.

By themselves, FIND and LEN aren't necessarily very useful, but you can use them in conjunction with other functions, such as LEFT and RIGHT, to extract or distribute text strings that aren't a uniform number of characters. For example:

```
=LEFT(B2,FIND(" ",B2))
```

will find the space in B2, and extract the characters preceding it beginning from the leftmost character in B2. Note that in this formula, the FIND function's `start_num` argument is omitted, so that the FIND function will begin at 1, the first character of the specified string.

To extract strings of varying lengths from the rightmost side of the string, you can use both the FIND and LEN functions within the RIGHT function. Here's an example:

```
=RIGHT(B2,(LEN(B2)-FIND(" ",B2)))
```

Here, the formula starts from the rightmost part of the string in B2. It will find (FIND) the space in the string, then subtract the position of the space from the length of the entire string (LEN), and return that many of the rightmost characters.

Note: when a function is used within another function as that function's argument, it is called a *nested function*.

Do it!

D-2:   Using functions to separate names

The files for this activity are in Student Data folder **Unit 1\Topic D**.

Here's how	Here's why
1 Click E2	You want to separate the employee names into two separate columns. You'll use the LEFT and FIND functions to extract the first names from column B to column E.
2 Type **=LEFT(B2,**	This part of the function dictates which text string you want to manipulate, and from which part of the string you want to extract a result.
3 Type **FIND(" ",B2))**	=LEFT(B2,FIND(" ",B2)) This part of the formula looks for the space within the text in B2, and will extract the characters from the leftmost part of the string up to and including the space.
Press ⏎ ENTER	To enter the formula. The result is Malcolm, the first name of the first employee in the list.
4 Copy the formula in E2 to E3:E20	
5 Click D2	You'll use the RIGHT, LEN, and FIND functions to separate out the last names into a new column.
6 Enter **=RIGHT(B2,(LEN(B2)-FIND(" ",B2)))**	
	This formula will extract text from the rightmost part of the string. The LEN function determines the length of the entire string in B2, and subtracts the position of the space (FIND) in the string. Because the `start_num` argument is omitted, the position of the space is 1.
Copy the formula in D2 to D3:D20	
7 Update and close the workbook	

Topic E: Date functions

Using date functions

Explanation

In Excel, dates are stored as sequential serial numbers. The serial number 1 is assigned to January 1, 1900. In this method, January 1, 2013 is serial number 41275. When a date is entered into a cell formatted as General, Excel automatically applies the Date format. For calculation purposes, the underlying value in the cell remains the serial number. To display the serial number in the cell, change the cell format to General or Number.

Excel provides a wide variety of built-in date functions that you can use to insert the current date in a cell or to calculate the number of days between the starting and ending dates. To insert a date function, click the Date & Time button in the Function Library group on the Formulas tab, and select the desired function. You can also click the Insert Function button to open the Insert Function dialog box.

TODAY

You use the TODAY function to enter the current date in the selected cell. The syntax is:

```
=TODAY()
```

YEAR

Use the YEAR function to return the year in the specified date serial number. Apply the General or Number format to the resulting value. The syntax for the YEAR function is:

```
=YEAR(serial_number)
```

You can also use this function to calculate the number of years between two dates. The formula would be:

```
=YEAR(serial_number)-YEAR(serial_number)
```

DAYS360

To calculate the number of days between a start date and an end date, use the DAYS360 function. This function is based on a 360-day year. The syntax for the DAYS360 function is:

```
=DAYS360(start_date,end_date)
```

To calculate the number of years between two dates, you can divide by 365 to get a more accurate result in years. If the resulting value is not a full year, then format the cell as Number to display the exact number of years with a decimal point. The syntax using the DAYS360 function would be:

```
=DAYS360(start_date,end_date)/365
```

NETWORKDAYS

You can use the NETWORKDAYS function to calculate the number of work days between the start date and the end date, excluding weekends. The Holidays argument is optional. The syntax is:

```
=NETWORKDAYS(start_date,end_date,[holidays])
```

Arguments in date functions

When entering arguments in the date functions, you can enter the date as *mm/dd/yyyy* and Excel will convert it to the serial number. If the date already appears in a cell, use the cell reference as the argument in the function.

Do it!

E-1:   Using date functions

The files for this activity are in Student Data folder **Unit 1\Topic E**.

Here's how	Here's why
1 Open HR dates.xlsx	In the current topic folder.
Save the workbook as **My HR dates.xlsx**	
2 On the Years of service worksheet, select E2	
Enter **=TODAY()**	The current date appears in Date format.
3 In E5, enter **=YEAR($E$2)-YEAR(D5)**	To calculate the number of years Davis Lee has been an employee. The answer looks odd because of the Date format.
Apply the **General** format to E5	To display the number of years of Davis Lee's employment.
4 Calculate the remaining employees' years of service	

Hire date	Years of service
1/20/1998	15
9/15/2010	3
2/2/2009	4
3/1/2013	0
4/8/1995	18

Drag the fill handle down from E5 to E32. For employees who were hired the same year as the current date, the years of service will be 0.

5 Update the workbook	
6 In F5, enter **=DAYS360(D5,$E$2)/365**	The DAYS360 function calculates the number of days between the hire date and the current date, based on a 360-day year. To find the number of years, you'll divide by 365. The result is formatted as a number with two decimal places.

7 Fill the formula down to E32

Years of service	
15	14.97
3	2.49
4	4.08
0	0.06
18	17.71

Employees who were hired in the current year will show years of service as a decimal number.

8 Update the workbook

9 Click the **Training phases** tab

This worksheet contains dates for training that occurs in three phases. You want to calculate the number of workdays being spent on training.

10 In D5, enter
    =NETWORKDAYS(B5,C5)

To calculate the number of actual workdays this time includes. The weekend days have been removed and the resulting number of days is 54.

Copy the formula to Phase II and Phase III

# of workdays
54
52
65

11 Observe H5:H12

This range contains the company holidays for the year 2012.

In E5, enter
=NETWORKDAYS(B5,C5,

You'll use the NETWORKDAYS function to calculate the number of workdays, excluding weekends and holidays.

Select H5:H12 and press (F4)

`=NETWORKDAYS(B5,C5,$H$5:$H$12`

To add the holiday argument as an absolute reference.

Press (↵ ENTER)

The number of days was reduced by 1 because the 1/2/2013 holiday fell within Phase I.

12 Copy the formula to Phase II and Phase III

workdays w/o holidays
53
51
62

Update and close the workbook

Topic F: Array formulas

Using array formulas

Explanation

The most basic definition of an *array* is a collection of values. Often, arrays are defined by cell references. However, arrays can also be groups of raw data or values. In this case, the arrays would be referred to as *array constants*.

An *array formula* performs multiple calculations on one or more sets of values, and then returns either a single result or multiple results. For example, as shown in Exhibit 1-5, you can create one array formula that calculates the Total sales for each product by multiplying the Unit price (B7:B19) by the Units sold (C7:C19) and entering the result in the range D7:D19. In this example, B7:B19 is an array, and C7:C19 is another array.

Creating array formulas

The syntax for array formulas is the same as any other Excel formula. You start with an equal sign (=), and you can use any built-in Excel function. You must press Ctrl+Shift+Enter to enter the formula. Array formulas are enclosed in braces {}. You cannot manually enter the braces to create an array formula.

D7	▼	:	✕	✓	f_x	{=B7:B19*C7:C19}		

	A	B	C	D
1	**Outlander Spices**			
2	**Inventory**			
3				
4				
5				
6	Product	Unit price	Units sold	Total Sales
7	Angelica Root	13.60	500	6800
8	Anise	3.34	2500	8350
9	Anise Seeds	19.54	430	8402.2
10	Annatto Seed	2.25	348	783
11	Asafoetida Powder	12.23	630	7704.9
12	Basil Leaf (Ground)	51.29	150	7693.5
13	Basil Leaf (Whole)	31.75	520	16510
14	Caraway Seed (Ground)	31.78	195	6197.1
15	Caraway Seed (Whole)	53.12	184	9774.08
16	Cardamom Seed (Ground)	24.37	190	4630.3
17	Cardamom Seed (Whole)	54.74	250	13685
18	Carob Powder (Raw)	1.50	855	1282.5
19	Cassia	9.87	580	5724.6
20				

Exhibit 1-5: Creating an array formula in D7:D19

Array formulas offer several advantages:

- **Consistency** — Because the same formula is entered in the destination range, verifying the accuracy of the formula is easier.

- **Editing safeguards** — When arrays involve multiple cells, you cannot edit just one of the cells. You must select the entire array, modify it, and then press Ctrl+Shift+Enter to confirm the change in the formula.

- **Reduced file size** — When a single array formula replaces multiple individual formulas, Excel needs to store only the single array formula. The more individual formulas replaced by the array formula, the greater the reduction in file size.

Do it!

F-1: Using an array formula

The files for this activity are in Student Data folder **Unit 1\Topic F**.

Here's how	Here's why
1 Open Inventory.xlsx	In the current topic folder.
Save the workbook as **My Inventory.xlsx**	
2 Select D7:D19	You will create an array that calculates the total sales for each product (Unit price*Units sold). The first step is to select the destination range.
3 Type **=B7:B19*C7:C19**	To multiply the unit prices by the units sold for each product. You can type or select the ranges B7:B19 and C7:C19.
4 Press (CTRL) + (SHIFT) + (↵ ENTER)	
	To enter the formula as an array formula. Excel encloses the array formula in braces. You can create an array formula only by pressing Ctrl+Shift+Enter; you cannot manually insert the braces.
5 Select the cells in D7:D19	{=B7:B19*C7:C19}
	If necessary. All cells contain the same array formula; however, the result of the calculation is different for each product.
6 Update the workbook	

Applying arrays to functions

Explanation

In addition to creating an array formula that returns multiple results, you can create an array formula that returns a single result, as shown in Exhibit 1-6. For example, you can use the SUM function to calculate the total sales of all products. In this case, you will use an array with the SUM function.

Use the following steps to create a SUM function using an array as the arguments:

1 Select the cell where you want the formula to be placed.

2 Type **=SUM(**

3 Enter (or select) the array to be used as the first argument.

4 Type *****

5 Enter (or select) the array to be used as the second argument. Type the closing parenthesis.

6 Press Ctrl+Shift+Enter.

B21	✕ ✓ *fx*	{=SUM(B7:B19*C7:C19)}		
	A	B	C	D
1	**Outlander Spices**			
2	**Inventory**			
3				
4				
5				
6	**Product**	**Unit price**	**Units sold**	**Total Sales**
7	Angelica Root	13.60	500	6800
8	Anise	3.34	2500	8350
9	Anise Seeds	19.54	430	8402.2
10	Annatto Seed	2.25	348	783
11	Asafoetida Powder	12.23	630	7704.9
12	Basil Leaf (Ground)	51.29	150	7693.5
13	Basil Leaf (Whole)	31.75	520	16510
14	Caraway Seed (Ground)	31.78	195	6197.1
15	Caraway Seed (Whole)	53.12	184	9774.08
16	Cardamom Seed (Ground)	24.37	190	4630.3
17	Cardamom Seed (Whole)	54.74	250	13685
18	Carob Powder (Raw)	1.50	855	1282.5
19	Cassia	9.87	580	5724.6
20				
21	Grand Total	$97,537.18		

Exhibit 1-6: Creating an array formula that returns a single result

Do it!

F-2:   Applying arrays to functions

Here's how	Here's why
1 Select B21	You will enter an array formula that calculations the grand total sales for the products.
2 Type **=SUM(B7:B19*C7:C19)**	To create a SUM function and use the array as the arguments.
3 Press (CTRL) + (SHIFT) + (↵ ENTER)	
	To create the array formula that will return a single result.
4 Observe the formula	The Grand Total in B21 is $97,537.18.
5 In D20, click Σ	To verify that the result is the same as the result in B21. Even though the range D7:D19 contains the array formula, the AutoSum function uses the values in its calculation.
Delete the formula in D20	
6 Update the workbook	

Modifying array formulas

Explanation

As stated earlier, you cannot delete or modify the contents of a cell that is included in a multi-cell array unless you edit the entire array. A common change is to add or remove rows that are included in the array formula. To do so, use the following technique:

1. Select the cell containing the array formula to be modified.
2. Press F2 to activate Edit mode. The braces temporarily disappear.
3. Edit the cell references as needed.
4. Press Ctrl+Shift+Enter to enter the modified array formula.

Do it!

F-3: Modifying the array formula

Here's how	Here's why
1 Move A21:B21 down to A29:B29	To make space to add more products.
2 Click the More products tab	This sheet contains eight additional products with unit price and units sold information that you want to include on the Inventory tab.
Copy A2:C9	You'll paste the information for the eight additional products into the Inventory sheet.
3 Click the Inventory tab	
Select A20 and paste the copied data	
4 Observe the error indicator in B29	

The formula in this cell refers to a range that has additional numbers adjacent to it.

	Excel recognizes that a change affecting the formula has occurred.
5 Press **F2**	To activate Edit mode as indicated in the status bar. The braces temporarily disappear as you edit the formula.
6 In the formula bar, change B19 to **B27**	To include the new products.
Change C19 to **C27**	The additional rows are included in the array arguments.
7 Press **CTRL** + **SHIFT** + **↵ ENTER**	
	To enter the modified array formula. The array formula is enclosed in braces again.

8 Select D7:D27

You must select the entire array to modify the array formula.

Activate Edit mode and change the cell references to **B27** and **C27**

Press F2, and edit the cell references in the formula bar.

9 Press (CTRL) + (SHIFT) + (↵ ENTER)

{=B7:B27*C7:C27}

To enter the modified array formula.

10 Update and close the workbook

Unit summary: Advanced functions and formulas

Topic A   In this topic, you used the **logical function IF** to evaluate a condition and return a value based on whether that condition is true or false. You also used the **IFERROR** function.

Topic B   In this topic, you used **conditional** functions to conditionally summarize, count, and average data.

Topic C   In this topic, you used the **PMT function** to calculate periodic payments for a loan.

Topic D   In this topic, you used **text** functions to manipulate strings of text in cells. You used the **LEFT**, **RIGHT**, and **MID** functions to extract specific numbers of characters from text strings, and you used the **FIND** and **LEN** functions to extract text from strings of varying lengths.

Topic E   In this topic, you used the **TODAY** and **NETWORKDAYS** functions to calculate differences between two dates.

Topic F   In this topic, you created an **array formula** that performed multiple calculations on multiple data sets to obtain multiple results. You also created an array formula using a SUM function.

Independent practice activity

In this activity, you'll use the IF function to calculate a commission rate. You'll then conditional functions to calculate sales data. Finally, you'll use text functions to separate column data.

The files for this activity are in Student Data folder **Unit 1\Unit summary**.

1 Open Functions practice.xlsx and save the workbook as My Functions practice.xlsx.

2 On the Commissions sheet, use the IF function to calculate a commission for each sales person by using the following criteria:

   • The commission rate for total sales over the sales goal in B4 is 3%.

   • The commission rate for total sales under the sales goal in B4 is 1%.

   (*Hint:* You can scroll down in the worksheet to see the formula for cell G8.) Compare your results to Exhibit 1-7.

3 On the Sales sheet, make the following conditional calculations:

   • In cell B27, sum the increase in sales over the target goal for stores in the East region.

   • In cell B28, calculate the number of stores in the East region that exceeded the target sales goal.

   • In cell B29, calculate the average increase in sales for those stores in the East region that exceeded the target goal.

   (*Hint:* Use SUMIFS, COUNTIFS, and AVERAGEIFS. Scroll down in the worksheet to see the correct formulas.) Compare your results to Exhibit 1-8.

4 Click the Products sheet. In B2, enter a function to separate the 4-character product code at the left part of the text string in A2. Copy the function to the B3:B12. (*Hint:* Use the LEFT function. Scroll down to A61 to see the correct formula.)

5 In C2, enter a function to separate the product name from the text string in A2. Copy the function to C3:C12. (*Hint:* Use the RIGHT, LEN, and FIND functions. Scroll down to A64 to see the correct formula.)

6 Update and close the workbook.

	A	B	C	D	E	F	G
1			Outlander Spices				
2			Commission report				
3							
4	Sales goal:	$8,500					
5							
6	Salesperson	Sales per quarter				Total sales	Commission
7		Qtr1	Qtr2	Qtr3	Qtr4		
8	Bill MacArthur	$2,500	$2,750	$3,500	$3,700	$7,450	$75
9	Jamie Morrison	$3,560	$3,000	$1,700	$2,000	$10,260	$308
10	Maureen O'Connor	$4,500	$4,000	$3,500	$3,700	$15,700	$471
11	Rebecca Austin	$3,250	$2,725	$3,000	$3,250	$12,225	$367
12	Paul Anderson	$2,520	$2,000	$2,500	$2,700	$9,720	$292
13	Cynthia Roberts	$1,500	$1,700	$1,800	$2,000	$7,000	$70
14	Rita Greg	$4,590	$4,050	$4,500	$3,700	$16,840	$505
15	Trevor Johnson	$3,660	$3,200	$3,000	$2,250	$12,110	$363
16	Kevin Meyers	$1,790	$1,800	$2,000	$2,200	$7,790	$78
17	Adam Long	$1,700	$1,950	$2,500	$2,750	$8,900	$267
18	Kendra James	$1,650	$2,000	$1,500	$1,750	$6,900	$69
19	Michael Lee	$2,050	$2,500	$2,800	$3,200	$10,550	$317
20	Sandra Lawrence	$3,425	$3,750	$4,000	$3,120	$14,295	$429
21	Mary Smith	$4,540	$2,700	$3,000	$3,200	$13,440	$403
22	Annie Philips	$1,200	$1,700	$1,800	$2,000	$6,700	$67

Exhibit 1-7: The calculated commissions after step 2

East Summary	
Increase above target	$6,985.00
Stores over target	2
Average increase	$3,492.50

Exhibit 1-8: The East Summary values after step 3

Review questions

1 What is the syntax of the IF function?

2 What date function inserts the current date?

3 What function inserts the current date and time?

4 How can you distinguish an array formula from a regular formula?

5 How do you enter an array formula?

Unit 2

Lookups and data tables

Complete this unit, and you'll know how to:

A Use the VLOOKUP and HLOOKUP functions to find values in a worksheet list.

B Use the MATCH function to find the relative position of a value in a range, and use the INDEX function to find the value of a cell at a given position within a range.

C Use data tables to see the effects of changing the values in a formula.

Topic A: Using lookup functions

Data lookups

Explanation

You can find a value in a range of related data in a worksheet by using *lookup functions*. These functions find a value in the first row or column of a list and then return a corresponding value from another row or column.

HLOOKUP and VLOOKUP

The HLOOKUP function performs a horizontal lookup. It finds values in a lookup table that has row labels in the leftmost column. The VLOOKUP function performs a vertical lookup. It finds values in a lookup table that has column labels in the topmost row.

HLOOKUP searches for the lookup value in the first row of the lookup table and returns a value in the same column from the specified row of the table. The syntax is:

```
HLOOKUP(lookup_value,table_array,row_index_num,range_lookup)
```

In this syntax:

- `lookup_value` is located in the first row of the lookup table.
- `table_array` is the name of the lookup table range.
- `row_index_num` is the number of the row from which a value will be returned.
- `range_lookup` is an optional argument that specifies whether you want HLOOKUP to find an exact or approximate match. You can specify FALSE if you want the function to search for a value that falls within a range, or specify TRUE if you want the function to search for an approximate match. If you omit the argument, HLOOKUP assumes that the value is TRUE.

Similarly, VLOOKUP searches for the lookup value in the first column of the lookup table and returns a value in the same row from the specified column of the table. The syntax is:

```
VLOOKUP(lookup_value,table_array,col_index_num,range_lookup)
```

In this syntax:

- `lookup_value` is located in the first column of the lookup table.
- `table_array` is the name of the lookup table range.
- `col_index_num` is the number of the column from which a value will be returned.
- `range_lookup` is an optional argument that specifies whether you want VLOOKUP to find an exact or approximate match. If you omit the argument, VLOOKUP assumes that the value is TRUE.

Do it!

A-1: Examining VLOOKUP

The files for this activity are in Student Data folder **Unit 2\Topic A**.

Here's how	Here's why
1 Open Employees.xlsx	In the current topic folder.
2 Save the workbook as **My Employees.xlsx**	This workbook contains four worksheets; Lookup is the active sheet. The data in the Lookup worksheet is sorted in ascending order by the values in the Employee ID column. The range A4:E6 contains a search box that currently displays the name and department for the employee identification number E001.
3 Verify that the Lookup sheet is active	
In A6, enter **E037**	The name and department details of Employee ID E037 appear in B6 and C6, respectively. Entering an incorrect identification number in A6 would create errors in B6 and C6.
4 Select B6	It contains a VLOOKUP function that finds the name of the employee whose identification number is specified in A6.
Observe the formula bar	`=VLOOKUP(A6,Emp_info,2,FALSE)`
	In this formula, "A6" refers to the cell containing the value that the function has to find. "Emp_info" is the range A10:F49, which constitutes the lookup table. The "2" refers to the table column from which the matching value is returned. "FALSE" indicates that the function must find an exact match.
	In the row containing E037, the value in the second column of the lookup table is Davis Lee.
5 Select C6	`=VLOOKUP(A6,Emp_info,5,FALSE)`
	It contains a VLOOKUP function that finds the department of the person whose employee identification number appears in A6.
6 Update the workbook	

Using VLOOKUP to find exact matches

Explanation

When you use the VLOOKUP function, remember the following:

- The lookup value must always be located in the first column of the lookup table.
- If the range_lookup argument is TRUE, the values in the first column of the lookup range must be in ascending order.
- Uppercase and lowercase text are equivalent.

Do it!

A-2:   Using VLOOKUP to find an exact match

Here's how	Here's why
1 Select D6	You'll use the VLOOKUP function to find the earnings of the employee whose ID is entered in A6.
Enter **=VLOOKUP(A6,Emp_info,6,FALSE)**	
	The value 72500 is returned.
2 In E6, enter **=VLOOKUP(A6,Emp_info,4,FALSE)**	
	The value East appears. This is the region of the employee whose ID is entered in A6.
3 In A6, enter **E029**	

Search	Results			
Employee ID	Name	Department	Earnings	Region
E029	Julie George	Marketing	130000	South

The employee details appear as shown.

4 Update the workbook

Using VLOOKUP to find approximate matches

Explanation

You can also use the VLOOKUP function to return an approximate match. To do this, specify the `range_lookup` argument as TRUE. If the function doesn't find an exact match, it looks for the largest value that is less than the lookup value and returns its corresponding data. This is also the default value if you leave the argument blank.

If the lookup value is less than the smallest value in the table, an error (#N/A) is returned.

Do it!

A-3: Using VLOOKUP to find an approximate match

Here's how	Here's why
1 Click the VLOOKUP sheet	This table lists discount percentages corresponding to purchase amounts. You'll find the nearest discount percentage based on an approximate matching lookup.
2 Select B6	You'll use the VLOOKUP function to find the discount percentage for the amount entered in A6. The table correlating purchase amounts to discounts is named Discount_table.
Enter **=VLOOKUP(A6,Discount_table,2,TRUE)**	Because the value in A6 is $1000, the lookup formula in B6 results in 3%, matching the data in the lookup table.
	You'll now enter a purchase amount value that doesn't appear in the table. The TRUE value in the last argument of the function tells VLOOKUP to look for an approximate match instead of an exact match.
3 In A6, enter **2500**	The discount for a $2000 purchase is 10%, and the discount for a $3500 purchase is 12%. The largest amount in the lookup table below your entry of $2500 is $2000, so the discount should be 10%. Because the VLOOKUP function is looking for an approximate match, it determines this and returns a discount value of 10%.
4 Update the workbook	

Using HLOOKUP to find exact matches

Explanation

HLOOKUP works like VLOOKUP except that it searches for values along a row instead of down a column. When you use the HLOOKUP function, remember the following:

- The lookup value must always be located in the first row of the lookup table.
- If the `range_lookup` argument is TRUE (approximate search), the values in the first row of the lookup range must be in ascending order.
- Uppercase and lowercase text are equivalent.

Do it!

A-4: Using HLOOKUP to find exact matches

Here's how	Here's why
1 Click the HLOOKUP-Exact sheet	You'll add formulas for horizontal lookups.
2 Select B5	A drop-down arrow appears.
3 Click the drop-down arrow and select **Qtr2**	Corresponding data is displayed in C5. The list ensures that you enter valid data.
4 Select C5	
Observe the formula	It is similar to the VLOOKUP formula, but it searches the first row in the table_array rather than the first column.
5 Select D5	
Enter **=HLOOKUP(B5,total_sales,9,FALSE)**	
	The row_index is 9, which is the row for Net profit. FALSE indicates a search for an exact match.
6 Select E5	
Enter the formula to show Profit % for the selected quarter	

Search	Profit Information		
Region	Gross Profit	Net Profit	% Profit
Qtr2	$36,150.00	$22,000.00	28.00%

The result appears as shown.

7 Update the workbook

Using HLOOKUP to find approximate matches

Explanation

You can also use the HLOOKUP function to return an approximate match. To do this, specify the `range_lookup` argument as TRUE. As with VLOOKUP, if the HLOOKUP function doesn't find an exact match, it looks for the largest value that is less than the lookup value and returns its corresponding data. This is also the default value if you leave the argument blank.

If the lookup value is less than the smallest value in the table, an error (#N/A) is returned. The data in the first row must be in ascending order. If it's not, the function might return unexpected results.

Do it!

A-5: Using HLOOKUP to find approximate matches

Here's how	Here's why
1 Click the HLOOKUP-Approx sheet	
2 Select C4	

	B	C
	Search	
	Earnings	Name
	$66,000	

You will enter an HLOOKUP function to find an approximate match.

Enter **=HLOOKUP(B4,base_salary,2,TRUE)**	TRUE indicates an approximate search. Sandy Stewart's earnings are the closest match to the value in B4.
3 Select B4	
Enter an amount between 60,000 and 80,000	You don't need to enter the comma or dollar sign. The function finds the largest value that is less than or equal to the entered value and returns the corresponding name.
Update and close the workbook	

Topic B: Using MATCH and INDEX

Explanation

The MATCH and INDEX functions are considered reference functions. You can use the MATCH function to determine the relative position of a value in a range. Conversely, the INDEX function returns a cell's value based on its relative position in a range. You can combine these two functions to obtain any information from any table.

The MATCH function

The syntax of the MATCH function is:

```
MATCH(lookup_value,lookup_array,match_type)
```

The arguments are:

- `lookup_value` — The value you want to find.
- `lookup_array` — The range of cells containing possible lookup values.
- `match_type` — An optional argument that can have the values 0, 1, or -1. If you want an exact match, use 0. If you want the function to search for the largest value that is less than or equal to the lookup value, use 1. If you want the function to search for the smallest value that is greater than or equal to the lookup value, use -1.

  If you use 1, the range should be sorted in ascending order. If you use -1, the range should be sorted in descending order. If you omit the argument, the function assumes that the value is 1.

Do it!

B-1: Using the MATCH function

The files for this activity are in Student Data folder **Unit 2\Topic B**.

Here's how	Here's why
1 Open Earnings.xlsx	In the current topic folder.
Save the workbook as **My Earnings.xlsx**	
2 Observe the Match and Index sheet	The data appears in ascending order of earnings. You'll use the MATCH function to find the relative position of a value in the selected range. The ranges A4:B7 and E4:F6 contain search boxes.
3 Select B6	(If necessary.) You'll find the relative position of "Sandy Stewart" in the column of names.
Enter **=MATCH(B5,Emp_name,0)**	In this formula, "B5" refers to the cell containing the lookup value. "Emp_name" refers to the range B10:B49, where the function searches for the lookup value. The "0" indicates that the values in the search range should match the lookup value exactly.
	The value 4 appears in B6. This is the relative position of "Sandy Stewart" in the column of names. In other words, her name is the fourth name in the list.
4 Select F6	You'll find the relative position of the value in F5 within the range F10:F49, named Earnings.
Enter **=MATCH(F5,Earnings,1)**	In this formula, "1" indicates that the function will find the largest value that is less than or equal to the lookup value.
	The relative position of the value in F5 appears as 24 in F6. The range named Earnings contains 24 values that are less than or equal to $100,000.
Observe the Earnings column	It doesn't contain the value $100,000. However, MATCH still displays a relative position in F6. This occurs because MATCH returns the relative position of the largest value that's less than or equal to $100,000.
5 Update the workbook	

The INDEX function

You can use the INDEX function if you want to find a value in a range by specifying a row number and a column number. The syntax of the INDEX function is:

    INDEX(range,row_num,col_num)

The arguments are:

- `range` — The group of cells in which to look for the value.

- `row_num` — The row from which a value will be returned. If the specified range contains only one row, you can omit the row number.

- `col_num` — The column from which a value will be returned. If the specified range contains only one column, you can omit the column number.

For example, `INDEX(A1:F10,4,6)` returns the value in row 4 and column 6 of the range A1:F10.

By itself, the INDEX function isn't very useful; the person looking for data isn't likely to know which row and column values to enter. When used with the MATCH function, however, the INDEX function can return values that the VLOOKUP function can't. VLOOKUP always looks for a matching value in the *leftmost* column of a data range. If you want to match a value in another column, you can use the MATCH function to return the row that matches the user's input, and then use that result in an INDEX function.

For example, in Exhibit 2-1, cell B6 contains a MATCH function to determine the row for the name entered in B5. Sandy Stewart is the fourth name in the Emp_info list. Cell B7 contains an INDEX function that looks in the row specified in B6 (in this case, row 4) and returns the value of the sixth column (Earnings, in this case, $65,000).

	A	B	C	D	E	F
1			**Outlander Spices**			
2			Employee information			
3						
4	Search based on name				Search based on earnings	
5	Enter name	Sandy Stewart			Enter earnings	$100,000
6	Relative position	4			Relative position	24
7	Earnings	$65,000				
8						
9	Employee identification number	Name	SSN	Region	Department	Earnings
10	E006	Annie Philips	000-85-8586	West	Human resources	$60,000
11	E030	Diana Stone	000-51-2998	East	Marketing	$60,000
12	E019	Jamie Morrison	000-35-4665	East	Human resources	$62,000
13	E033	Sandy Stewart	000-39-8005	East	Marketing	$65,000
14	E014	Michael Lee	000-87-9898	North	Sales	$68,000
15	E031	Rob Dukes	000-64-6797	West	Accounts	$70,000
16	E001	Malcolm Pingault	000-17-3312	East	Human resources	$72,000
17	E037	Davis Lee	000-28-7743	East	Accounts	$72,500
18	E036	Nikki Cleary	000-06-7767	South	Administraion	$75,000
19	E032	Tammy Heiret	000-76-8988	West	Customer support	$76,000
20	E040	Sonia McCormick	000-75-7878	East	Administration	$78,000
21	E002	Shannon Lee	000-70-8097	South	Accounts	$80,000

Exhibit 2-1: The INDEX function used with the MATCH function

Do it!

B-2: Using the INDEX function

Here's how	Here's why
1 Observe B7	You want to display the salary for the employee whose name is entered in cell B5. You can't use the VLOOKUP function for this because the person's name is in the second column of the data table, not the first column.
	You'll begin by experimenting with the INDEX function, which you'll use to solve this problem.
2 Select B7	You'll enter row and column values directly into the formula this time to see how the INDEX function works.
Enter **=INDEX(Emp_info,2,6)**	In this formula, "Emp_info" refers to the range A10:F49. The "2" and "6" refer to the row and column from which the function should return a value.
	The value $60,000 appears in B7. This is the value from the second row and sixth column of the specified range.
	You'll now replace the number 2 with the value from cell B6, which represents the row of the entered name (calculated by using the MATCH function).
3 Select B7	
Edit the formula to read **=INDEX(Emp_info,B6,6)**	As shown in Exhibit 2-1, the value $65,000 appears in B7. Because B6 contains the value 4 (the row number for Sandy Stewart), the value in column 6 that the INDEX function returns is her salary.
4 Select B5	You'll verify that the functions work when you enter a different name.
Enter **Davis Lee**	

Search based on name	
Enter name	Davis Lee
Relative position	8
Earnings	$72,500

The MATCH function in B6 calculates the relative position of 8, and the INDEX function in B7 calculates the salary of $72,500.

5 Update and close the workbook

Topic C: Creating data tables

Data tables

Explanation

A *data table* is a range that displays the results of changing certain values in one or more formulas. The different values you want to enter in a formula are also included in the data table. A data table can have either a single variable or two variables.

One-variable data tables

You can use a one-variable data table to observe the effects of changing one variable in one or more formulas. For example, you can see how changing the interest rate affects monthly payments by using the PMT function:

    PMT(A5%/12,36,12000)

In this function, A5 is called the *input cell*, where various input values are substituted from the data table.

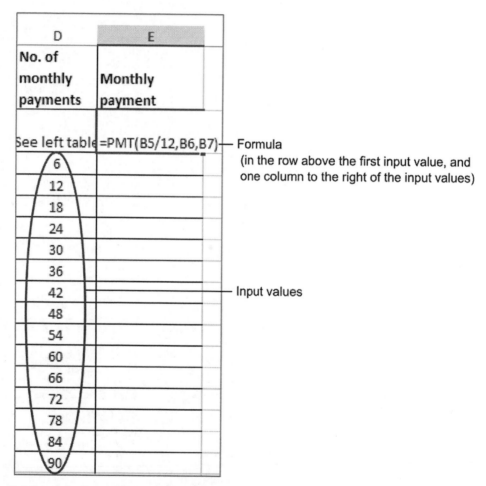

Exhibit 2-2: Creating a one-variable data table

To create a one-variable data table:

1 Enter input values in a row or a column.

2 If you list the input values in a column, then enter the formula in the cell located at the intersection of the row above the first input value and the column to the right of the input values, as shown in Exhibit 2-2. If you list the input values in a row, then enter the formula in the cell located at the intersection of the column to the left of the first value and the row just below the row of input values.

3 Select the range containing the input values and the formula.

4 On the Data tab, in the Data Tools group, click What-If Analysis and choose Data Table to open the Data Table dialog box.

5 If the input values are in a column, specify the input cell in the Column input cell box. If the input values are in a row, use the Row input cell box.

6 Click OK.

Do it!

C-1:   Creating a one-variable data table

The files for this activity are in Student Data folder **Unit 2\Topic C**.

Here's how	Here's why
1 Open Payments.xlsx	In the current topic folder.
Save the workbook as **My Payments.xlsx**	
2 Click the 1v data table sheet	(If necessary.) You'll create a one-variable data table to analyze payments. D6:E21 will form the data table. The range D7:D21 contains the input values you'll use while creating the data table.
3 In E6, enter **=PMT(B5/12,B6,B7)**	To calculate monthly payments based on the input cell. The value -8,791.59 appears.
4 Select D6:E21	
5 Click the **Data** tab	
In the Data Tools group, click the arrow on the What-If Analysis button and choose **Data Table...**	What-If Analysis ▾ Scenario Manager... Goal Seek... Data Table...
	To open the Data Table dialog box.
6 Place the insertion point in the Column input cell box	
Select B6	(In the worksheet.) This is the cell where the list of column input values from the data table will be substituted.

7 Click **OK**

Payment analysis	
No. of monthly payments	Monthly payment
See left table	-8,791.59
6	-17,156.14
12	-8,791.59
18	-6,005.71
24	-4,614.49
30	-3,781.14
36	-3,226.72
42	-2,831.68
48	-2,536.26
54	-2,307.24
60	-2,124.70
66	-1,975.97
72	-1,852.58
78	-1,748.69
84	-1,660.12
90	-1,583.79

(In the Data Table dialog box.) E6:E21 shows how different values for "No. of monthly payments" affect the monthly payment for the loan amount in B7. Because 12 appears in both the initial formula and the data table, the payment value of -8,791.59 appears twice.

You can change the initial value used in the formula without affecting the data table.

In B6, enter **10**

The value in E6 (at the top of the data table) changes to -10,464.04, but the rest of the table values remain.

8 Update the workbook

Two-variable data tables

Explanation

You can use a two-variable data table to see the effect of changing two variables in one or more formulas, as shown in Exhibit 2-3. For example, you can see how changing the interest rate and the number of payments affect a monthly payment.

To create a two-variable data table:

1   Enter a formula that contains two input cells.
2   Below the formula (in the same column), enter the first list of input values. To the right of the formula (in the same row), enter the second list of input values.
3   Select the range containing both the input values and the formula.
4   In the Data Tools group, click What-If Analysis arrow and choose Data Table to open the Data Table dialog box.
5   In the Row input cell box, specify the row input cell.
6   In the Column input cell box, specify the column input cell.
7   Click OK.

PMT function	Column input values (below the formula)			Row input values (to the right of the formula)			
=PMT(B4/12,B5,B6)	9%	10%	11%	12%	13%	14%	15%
6							
12							
18							
24							
30							
36							
42							
48							
54							
60							
66							
72							
78							
84							
90							

Exhibit 2-3: A two-variable data table

Do it!

C-2: Creating a two-variable data table

Here's how	Here's why
1 Click the 2v data table sheet	You'll create a two-variable data table to analyze monthly payments.
2 In B7, enter **=PMT(B4/12,B5,B6)**	To calculate monthly payments based on two input cells.
3 Select B7:I22	
Open the Data Table dialog box	(Click What-If Analysis arrow and choose Data Table.) The insertion point is in the Row input cell box.
4 Select B4	

To specify the row input cell.

Place the insertion point in the Column input cell box	
Select B5	

To specify the column input cell.

5 Click **OK**	C8:I22 shows how different numbers of months and different interest rates affect the monthly payments for the loan amount in B6.
6 In B6, enter **250000**	The data table now shows payments based on a loan amount of $250,000.
7 Update and close the workbook	

Unit summary: Lookups and data tables

Topic A   In this topic, you learned that lookup functions are used to find specific values in a worksheet. You used the **VLOOKUP** function to search for a value in a list that is arranged vertically, and you used the **HLOOKUP** function to search for a value in a list that is arranged horizontally.

Topic B   In this topic, you used the **MATCH** function to find the relative position of a value in a range. You used the **INDEX** function to find a value in a range by specifying row and column numbers. You also used these two functions together to look up information more flexibly than you can with the VLOOKUP function.

Topic C   In this topic, you learned that a **data table** displays the effects of changing the values in a formula. You used a **one-variable** data table to observe the effect of changing one variable in a formula. You then used a **two-variable** data table to observe the effect of changing two variables in a formula.

Review questions

1 True or false? The VLOOKUP function is a vertical lookup function that finds values in a lookup table that has row labels in the leftmost column.

2 What is the syntax of the VLOOKUP function?

3 List three important points to remember about using the VLOOKUP function.

4 What is the purpose of the MATCH function?

5 What is a data table?

Independent practice activity

In this activity, you'll use the VLOOKUP function to search for a value in a list that is arranged vertically. You'll also use the MATCH function, and you'll create a one-variable data table.

The files for this activity are in Student Data folder **Unit 2\Unit summary**.

1 Open City managers.xlsx. Verify that Lookup is the active worksheet.

2 Save the workbook as **My City managers.xlsx**.

3 In B6, enter the VLOOKUP function that finds the manager of the city entered in A6. In C6, enter the VLOOKUP function that finds the phone number of the same manager. (*Hint:* The lookup table is named Contact_list. Scroll down to cell A100 to see the correct formulas for B6 and C6.) Compare your results to Exhibit 2-4.

4 Click the Match worksheet. In B6, use the MATCH function to find the number of managers with fewer accounts than the value entered in A6. (*Hint:* The accounts column is named Num_accounts. Scroll down to cell A100 to see the correct formula for B6.) Compare your results to Exhibit 2-5.

5 Click the 1v data table worksheet. In F6:G21, create a one-variable data table to calculate the monthly payments for the various payment schedules in F7:F21. Use the PMT function with an annual interest rate of 10%. Compare your results with Exhibit 2-6. (*Hint:* Scroll down to cell A100 to see the correct formula for G6.)

6 Update and close the workbook.

Outlander Spices		
City managers details		
Search	Results	
Enter city	Manager name	Phone number
Seattle	Shannon Lee	(555) 116-1111

Exhibit 2-4: The results of the VLOOKUP function in Step 3

Outlander Spices	
City managers details	
Search	Results
Enter # of accounts	Number of managers with fewer than target
20	5

Exhibit 2-5: The results of the MATCH function in Step 4

Payment analysis	
No. of monthly payments	Monthly deduction
See left table	-728.55
6	-2,081.21
12	-1,066.51
18	-728.55
24	-559.78
30	-458.69
36	-391.43
42	-343.51
48	-307.67
54	-279.89
60	-257.75
66	-239.70
72	-224.74
78	-212.13
84	-201.39
90	-192.13

Exhibit 2-6: The results obtained after Step 5

Unit 3

Advanced data management

Complete this unit, and you'll know how to:

A Use the data validation feature to validate data entered in cells.

B Use the Custom AutoFilter and Advanced Filter dialog boxes to filter data based on complex criteria.

Topic A: Validating cell entries

Validating data

Explanation

You can use Excel's data validation feature to ensure that selected cells accept only valid data, such as text, dates, or whole numbers. You can also ensure that users select only valid values from a specified list of options.

Validating data ensures that data entries match a specified format. You can display an input message that prompts users for the correct entries, and display a specific error message when incorrect data is entered.

To quickly see invalid data, you can display circles around invalid entries. To do so, click the Data tab, click the Data Validation arrow, and choose Circle Invalid Data. To remove the circles, click the Data Validation arrow and choose Clear Validation Circles.

Do it!

A-1: Observing data validation

The files for this activity are in Student Data folder **Unit 3\Topic A**.

Here's how	Here's why
1 Open Details.xlsx	The Observing data validation sheet is active. You'll observe the cells in which only certain kinds of data can be entered.
2 Save the workbook as **My Details.xlsx**	In the current topic folder.
3 Verify that the Observing data validation sheet is active	
4 Select B7, as shown	

Name	Emp_Id	Date of hire
Adam Long	E001	12/1/1997
Paul Anderson	E002	4/1/1998
Shannon Lee	✛	

Emp_Id
Employee identification number should be four characters long.

An input message appears, stating the acceptable format for Emp_Id numbers.

5 Enter **E1234**

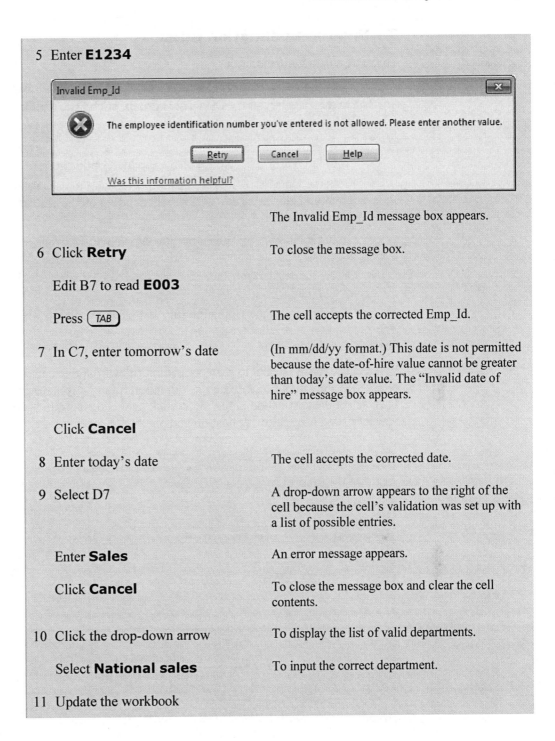

The Invalid Emp_Id message box appears.

6 Click **Retry**   To close the message box.

   Edit B7 to read **E003**

   Press (TAB)   The cell accepts the corrected Emp_Id.

7 In C7, enter tomorrow's date   (In mm/dd/yy format.) This date is not permitted
                                          because the date-of-hire value cannot be greater
                                          than today's date value. The "Invalid date of
                                          hire" message box appears.

   Click **Cancel**

8 Enter today's date   The cell accepts the corrected date.

9 Select D7   A drop-down arrow appears to the right of the
                                          cell because the cell's validation was set up with
                                          a list of possible entries.

   Enter **Sales**   An error message appears.

   Click **Cancel**   To close the message box and clear the cell
                                          contents.

10 Click the drop-down arrow   To display the list of valid departments.

   Select **National sales**   To input the correct department.

11 Update the workbook

Setting data validation rules

Explanation

To create a data validation rule:

1 Select the cells for which you want to create a validation rule.
2 On the Data tab, in the Data Tools group, click Data Validation to open the Data Validation dialog box, shown in Exhibit 3-1.
3 Click the Settings tab.
4 From the Allow list, select a data validation option.
5 From the Data list, select the operator you want to use. Then complete the remaining entries. (They will vary depending on the validation option and operator selected.)
6 On the Input Message tab, enter the message to be displayed when users select the cell.
7 On the Error Alert tab, enter the message to be displayed when users enter invalid data.
8 Click OK to set the validation rule and close the dialog box.

Pasting validation rules

You can use Paste Special to paste validation rules from one cell or range to another. To do so, select the range containing the validation rule you want to copy and click Copy. Then select the destination range, right-click, and choose Paste Special. In the Paste Special dialog box, select Validation and click OK.

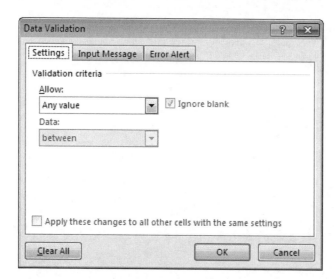

Exhibit 3-1: The Data Validation dialog box

Do it!

A-2: Creating a data validation rule

Here's how	Here's why
1 Click the Setting up data validation sheet	
2 Select B5	You'll create a validation rule to ensure that employee numbers are four characters long.
3 In the Data Tools group, click **Data Validation**	(On the Data tab.) To open the Data Validation dialog box, shown in Exhibit 3-1. By default, the Settings tab is active.
4 From the Allow list, select **Text length**	Allow: Any value Any value Whole number Decimal List Date Time Text length Custom You will specify the number of characters permitted in each cell of the selected range. The Data list and the Minimum and Maximum boxes appear in the dialog box. The Ignore blank option also becomes available.
From the Data list, select **equal to**	To specify the comparison operator. The Length box replaces the Minimum and Maximum boxes.
In the Length box, enter **4**	Allow: Text length Data: equal to Length: 4 To specify the number of characters permitted.

5 Click the Input Message tab	You'll specify the message that will appear when users select a cell in the Emp_Id column.
In the Title box, enter **Emp_Id**	This text will appear as a title in the input message.
In the Input message box, enter **Employee ID should be four characters long.**	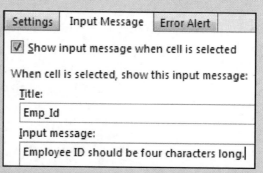
	This message will appear when the user selects a cell.
6 Click the Error Alert tab	
In the Title box, enter **Invalid Emp_Id**	This will be the title of the error message box.
In the Error message box, enter **The employee ID number you've entered is not permitted. Please enter another value.**	This is the error message that will appear when the user enters an invalid employee identification number.
7 Display the Style list, as shown	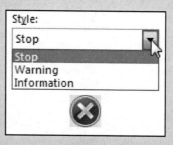
	To see the three types of error messages: Stop, Warning, and Information. Each error alert has its own corresponding icon.
Close the Style list	To leave the error alert style as Stop.
Click **OK**	To set the validation rule.
8 Observe **B5**	The input message appears.
9 Enter **103**	The Invalid Emp_Id message box appears because you entered only three characters.
Click **Retry**	Or press Enter.
Enter **E103**	

10 Right-click B5 and choose **Copy**

   Select B6:B20

   Right-click and choose
   Paste Special...

   Under Paste, select **Validation**

   Click **OK**   The validation rule has been copied to the
                                    remaining cells in column B. You can verify the
                                    rule by selecting any cell and observing the
                                    input message.

11 Update the workbook

Using date and list criteria in data validation rules

Explanation

In addition to using text-length data validation, you can use date and list criteria in your data validation rules.

To specify date criteria for valid data:

1 Select the cells you want to validate.

2 On the Data tab, click Data Validation.

3 On the Settings tab in the Data Validation dialog box, select Date from the Allow list.

4 From the Data list, select the operator you want to use.

5 Complete the remaining criteria entries. When specifying dates, you can enter formulas that return dates, such as =TODAY().

   Note: The TODAY function returns the current date; the NOW function returns the current date and time.

6 Define an input message and an error message, if desired.

7 Click OK.

To specify list criteria for valid data:

1 Select the cells you want to validate.

2 Open the Data Validation dialog box.

3 On the Settings tab, select List from the Allow list.

4 In the Source box, enter the desired list items, separated by a comma. List items are case sensitive. To edit items in the Source box, use the Backspace key or click the mouse.

   Note: You can also enter a cell or range reference instead of typing the list items.

5 Define an input message and an error message, if desired.

6 Click OK.

The width of the cell containing the data validation rule determines the width of the drop-down list. You can increase the width of the cell to make sure that longer items are completely visible in the drop-down list.

Do it!

A-3:   Setting date and list validation rules

Here's how	Here's why
1 Select C5:C20	You'll create a validation rule to ensure that the date of hire entered is on or before today's date.
Open the Data Validation dialog box	Click Data Validation in the Data Tools group.
2 Click the **Settings** tab	
3 Enter the validation criteria as shown	Validation criteria Allow: Date Data: less than or equal to End date: =TODAY()
Click **OK**	To set the validation.
4 In C5, enter tomorrow's date	(In mm/dd/yy format.) An error message appears.
Click **Retry**	Or press Enter.
Enter a valid date of hire	A date earlier than or equal to today's date.
5 Select D5:D20	You'll create a list of valid departments from which the user can choose.
Click **Data Validation**	The Settings tab is active.
6 From the Allow list, select **List**	
In the Source box, enter **Accounting, Customer Service, Human Resources, Marketing, National Sales**	Validation criteria Allow: List ☑ Ign Data: ☑ In-c less than or equal to Source: esources, Marketing, National Sales
	To create the list of values for the column. If the list of values appeared in the worksheet, you could enter the range in the Source box.
Click **OK**	To set the validation rule. A drop-down arrow appears to the right of D5.

7 In D5, click the drop-down arrow

Department	▼
Accounting	
Customer Service	
Human Resources	
Marketing	
National Sales	

To display the list you just created.

Select **Marketing**

8 Update and close the workbook

Topic B: Advanced filtering

Custom AutoFilters

Explanation

You can filter data based on two or more criteria by using Excel's advanced filtering features. For example, you can display the records of all employees whose department is either Marketing or Sales. Excel provides the Custom AutoFilter and Advanced Filter tools for specifying multiple filtering criteria.

Use the Custom AutoFilter dialog box to specify multiple criteria for the same column heading, as shown in Exhibit 3-2.

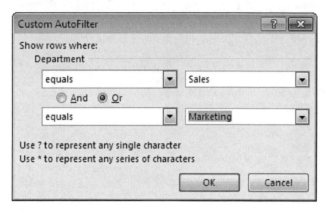

Exhibit 3-2: The Custom AutoFilter dialog box

In Exhibit 3-2, Department is the column on which the data will be filtered. The first criterion states that the department must be Sales; the second criterion states that the department must be Marketing. The two criteria are joined by the Or operator, meaning that rows will be included in the filtered data if they meet *either* criterion. When you use the And operator, the rows must meet *both* criteria. The criteria shown in Exhibit 3-2 would yield all employees who work in either the Sales or Marketing departments.

To filter data by using the Custom AutoFilter dialog box:

1 Turn on AutoFilter.

2 Display the drop-down menu for the column for which you want to create criteria. Then choose Text Filters, Custom Filter to open the Custom AutoFilter dialog box.

3 Select the first comparison operator and its associated criterion.

4 Select And or Or. By selecting And, you'll decrease the number of rows that meet the criteria. By selecting Or, you'll increase the number of matching rows.

5 Select the second comparison operator and its associated criterion.

6 Click OK.

Do it!

B-1:   Using Custom AutoFilter criteria

The files for this activity are in Student Data folder **Unit 3\Topic B**.

Here's how	Here's why
1 Open Employees.xlsx	In the current topic folder.
Save the workbook as **My Employees.xlsx**	
2 Click **Filter**	To enable filtering.
Click the AutoFilter arrow next to Department	To display the sorting and filtering criteria. You'll display the records of those employees who belong to either the Sales department or the Marketing department.
3 Choose **Text Filters**, **Custom Filter...**	To open the Custom AutoFilter dialog box. In the upper-left list, the first comparison operator, equals, is selected.
From the upper-right list, select **Sales**	

Show rows where:
Department

| equals ▼ | Sales ▼ |

◉ And   ○ Or

	To specify the first comparison criterion.
Select **Or**	This tells Excel to display all records that match either of the two comparison criteria.
4 From the lower-left list, select **equals**	To specify the second comparison operator.
From the lower-right list, select **Marketing**	To specify the second comparison criterion. The Custom AutoFilter dialog box should look like Exhibit 3-2.
Click **OK**	The worksheet displays 14 records of employees who work in either the Sales department or the Marketing department.
5 In the Sort & Filter group, click **Clear**	The data is no longer filtered by these two criteria. AutoFilter remains active.

Creating a criteria range

Explanation

You can filter records based on two or more column headings by using multiple criteria. For example, you can filter data to display the records of all East region employees whose salaries are greater than $100,000, and all West region employees whose salaries are greater than or equal to $80,000. A criteria range filters data based on complex criteria.

A *criteria range* is a cell range containing a set of search conditions. It consists of one row of criteria labels and at least one row that defines the search conditions. Each criterion label must be the name of a column for which you want to specify a criterion. The Advanced Filter dialog box filters a range of data according to a criteria range.

The following table lists the comparison operators that can be used in a criteria range:

Operator	Meaning
=	Equal to
>	Greater than
<	Less than
>=	Greater than or equal to
<=	Less than or equal to
<>	Not equal to

To create a criteria range by using the Advanced Filter dialog box:

1 Enter at least one criterion label in a cell that is *not* adjacent to the range containing the data. The criterion label must be exactly the same as the column heading in the data range.

2 Below the cell that contains the criterion label, enter a comparison criterion.

3 Click the Data tab.

4 In the Sort & Filter group, click Advanced to open the Advanced Filter dialog box.

5 In the List range box, enter the range you want to filter. The range must include the associated column headings.

6 In the Criteria range box, enter the range that contains your criteria.

7 Click OK.

	A	B	C	D	E	F
3	Name	Emp code	Empl #	Region	Department	Earning ($)
15	Wendy Alto	34	43-730	East	Administration	105000
18	Paul Anderson	11	43-133	East	Human resources	180000
19	Rita Greg	9	42-800	East	Sales	380050
20	Kendra James	16	16-111	East	Sales	144000
35	Kevin Meyers	17	16-656	West	Accounts	84000
36	Maureen O'Connor	20	42-212	West	Accounts	120000
37	Pamela Carter	25	43-517	West	Accounts	84000
38	Anna Morris	26	16-162	West	Accounts	150000
39	Rita Lawson	27	42-521	West	Accounts	106000
40	Tina Ralls	35	16-497	West	Administration	124000
41	Julia Stockton	39	43-283	West	Customer support	96600
42	James Owens	24	16-871	West	Marketing	92000
43	Cynthia Roberts	13	43-129	West	Sales	136000

Exhibit 3-3: The data with an advanced filter consisting of two criteria

Do it!

B-2:   Using the Advanced Filter dialog box

Here's how	Here's why
1 In H3, enter **Region**	To specify the first criterion label. Ensure that it exactly matches the column heading in the data range. Copying and pasting the column headings is a good way to ensure that the labels are identical to those in the data range.
In I3, enter **Earning ($)**	To specify the second criterion label. Be sure to include the space between *Earning* and *($)*. (You can copy and paste the heading from F3.)
2 In H4, enter **East**	To specify East as the first comparison criterion.
In I4, enter **>100000**	To complete the first row of criteria. These criteria will display only those values in the East region with earnings greater than $100,000.
3 In H5, enter **West**	To specify West as the criterion.
In I5, enter **>=80000**	The second row of the criteria range will display values in the West region with earnings greater than or equal to $80,000. Adding rows to a criteria range amounts to using an Or operator, so rows will be included if they meet either of these conditions.

4	Select any cell in the original data range	(In the range A4:F43.) You'll enter the entire data range automatically when you choose the Advanced Filter command.
	In the Sort & Filter group, click **Advanced**	To open the Advanced Filter dialog box. "Filter the list, in-place" is selected by default. This means that the filtered data will be displayed in the same worksheet. The entire data range appears selected in the worksheet.
5	Collapse the Criteria range box	(Click the Collapse Dialog button.) The Advanced Filter - Criteria range: dialog box appears.
	Select H3:I5	

Region	Earning ($)
East	>100000
West	>=80000

To enter the criteria range.

6	Expand the Criteria range box	The Advanced Filter dialog box expands.
	Click **OK**	As shown in Exhibit 3-3, the records of the four employees in the East region whose salaries are greater than $100,000 are displayed, as well as the records of the nine employees in the West region whose salaries are greater than or equal to $80,000.
7	Display the unfiltered data	Click Clear in the Sort & Filter group.
8	Update the workbook	

Copy filtered results to another location

Explanation

In the examples you've seen so far, rows are filtered out of the data so that all you can see are the remaining rows. You can also choose to keep the original data intact and place a copy of the filtered data somewhere else in the same worksheet or in another worksheet in the workbook. To do so, select the "Copy to another location" option in the Advanced Filter dialog box, and then specify a starting cell for the copied data, as shown in Exhibit 3-4.

Exhibit 3-4: Copying filtered data to another location

Do it!

B-3: Copying filtered results to another range

Here's how	Here's why
1 Select a cell in the Name column	If necessary.
2 Open the Advanced Filter dialog box	(Click Advanced in the Sort & Filter group.) The list and criteria ranges that were previously entered in the dialog box are still there.
3 Select **Copy to another location**	The Copy to box is enabled.
Place the insertion point in the Copy to box	
Select H10	This cell will be the starting point for the filtered result. The dialog box should look like Exhibit 3-4.
4 Click **OK**	The worksheet displays the filtered data in the specified location.
Update and close the workbook	

Unit summary: Advanced data management

Topic A

In this topic, you learned that **data validation** ensures the entry of valid information in a worksheet. You specified a set of rules to validate data. You also specified input messages and error messages to be displayed to prompt the user to enter correct data.

Topic B

In this topic, you used the **Custom AutoFilter** dialog box to filter data based on multiple criteria. You used a criteria range and the **Advanced Filter** command to specify more complex criteria. You also copied filtered data to another location in the worksheet.

Review questions

1 What's the purpose of validating data?

2 List the steps you would use to set data validation rules.

3 What is a criteria range?

4 List the steps you would use to keep an original range of data intact and place a copy of the filtered data somewhere else in the same worksheet.

Independent practice activity

In this activity, you'll perform calculations by using several Excel functions. You'll also create data validation rules and use the DCOUNT function.

The files for this activity are in Student Data folder **Unit 3\Unit summary**.

1 Open Data management.xlsx, and ensure that the Data validation worksheet is active.

2 Save the workbook as **My Data management.xlsx**.

3 Create a data validation rule to accept only those Store codes with lengths between four and six characters and residing in the range A5:A24. (*Hint:* Data Validation is in the Data Tools group on the Data tab.)

4 For the range B5:B24, create a list of regions from which users can choose. The list should contain **East**, **North**, **South**, and **West**. Also, ensure that a proper error message appears when the user enters an invalid region.

5 Create a data validation rule to ensure that the range C5:C24 accepts only whole numbers greater than zero.

6 Test your new data validation rules. Make any necessary adjustments.

7 Click the Adv. filter worksheet tab. Use the criteria labels in F3:G3 to create a criteria range to display only those records where the re-order level for Cedric Stone is greater than 2000, or the re-order level for Bill Johnson is greater than 3000. (*Hint:* In F4, enter **Cedric Stone**; in G4, enter **>2000**; and so on. Select a cell in the original range and click Advanced in the Sort & Filter group. Select F3:G5 as the criteria range.)

8 Copy the filtered result to a range starting with I3 so that you can view the filtered and unfiltered data simultaneously. (*Hint:* Open the Advanced Filter dialog box and select "Copy to another location.")

9 Adjust column widths and row heights as necessary in the resulting range, and compare your results with Exhibit 3-5.

10 Update and close the workbook.

I	J	K	L
Product name	Product code	Suppliers	Re-order level(Kg)
Anise	32	Cedric Stone	2500
Caraway seed (ground)	14	Bill Johnson	3200
Cardamom seed (ground)	5	Cedric Stone	4000

Exhibit 3-5: The results after step 9

Unit 4

Advanced charting

Complete this unit, and you'll know how to:

A Adjust the scale of a chart, and format data points.

B Create combination charts, trendlines, and sparklines to highlight different kinds of data.

C Insert and format graphical objects in charts.

Topic A: Chart formatting options

Changing a chart's scale

Explanation

Excel provides many formatting options for charts. You can use these options to represent or interpret complex data. For example, you can change the scale of a chart or format specific data points.

When you create or work with a chart, the Chart Tools appear. Design and Format tabs are added to the ribbon.

You can change the scale of a chart to:

- Adjust the range of values on each axis.
- Change the way the values appear on each axis.
- Specify the intervals at which the values appear.
- Set the point at which one axis crosses another.

To change the scale of a chart, select the value axis and click the Format tab. In the Current Selection group, click Format Selection to open the Format Axis task pane, as shown in. Exhibit 4-1.

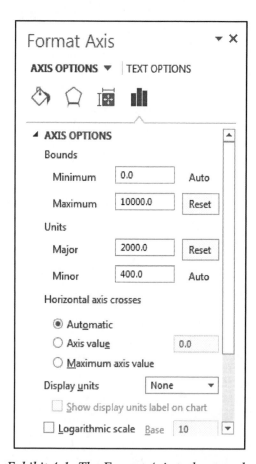

Exhibit 4-1: The Format Axis task pane, showing options for the vertical value axis

The following table describes some of the options on the Axis Options pane:

Option	Specifies
Minimum	The lowest value on the value axis.
Maximum	The highest value on the value axis.
Major unit	The intervals for major tick marks and major gridlines on the value axis.
Minor unit	The intervals for minor tick marks and minor gridlines on the value axis.

Do it!

A-1: Adjusting the scale of a chart

The files for this activity are in Student Data folder **Unit 4\Topic A**.

Here's how	Here's why
1 Open Yearly bonus.xlsx	From the current topic folder.
Save the workbook as **My Yearly bonus.xlsx**	
2 Verify that the Scale worksheet is active	It contains the quarterly bonus sales report for five Outlander Spices salespeople.
3 Observe the chart	

The vertical value axis displays a maximum value of $15,000. The interval between the values is $5,000. This scale is not suitable because the value axis is too large, making the columns seem small and minimizing the difference between data points.

4 Click to select the vertical value axis, as shown	
	The Chart Tools appear on the ribbon.

5 Click the Format tab	On the ribbon.
In the Current Selection group, verify that **Vertical (Value) Axis** is selected	
Click Format Selection	To open the Format Axis task pane.
6 In the task pane, under Bounds, edit the Maximum box to read **10000**	Excel might reformat the values here with a single decimal place. The value you enter might appear as 10000.0.
Set the Major unit to **2000**	

Bounds

Minimum	0.0
Maximum	10000.0

Units

Major	2000.0
Minor	400.0

7 Close the Format Axis task pane	To apply the new scale settings.
Deselect the chart	

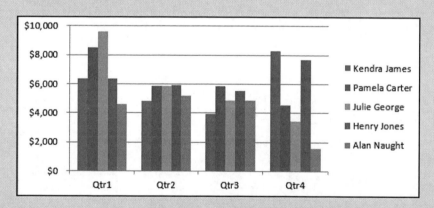

The value axis now displays a maximum value of $10,000. The major tick marks occur at intervals of $2,000. This scale is more appropriate for the data.

8 Update the workbook

Formatting data points

Explanation

You can change the appearance of data points to make them stand out or make them easier to understand. You can add or remove labels, percentages, or leader lines. (A *leader line* is a line from the data label to its associated data point.) In a pie chart, you can change the orientation of the first slice or pull out a slice to make it stand out.

Labeling data points

To add a label to a data point:

1 Select the data point you want to label.
2 Click the Format tab.
3 In the Current Selection group, click Format Selection to open the Format Data Point dialog box.
4 Click Label Options to display the corresponding page, as shown in Exhibit 4-2.
5 Select a label option and click Close.

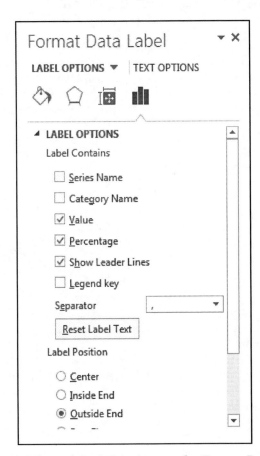

Exhibit 4-2: Label options in the Format Data Label task pane

Formatting pie charts

You can format a pie chart to draw attention to specific data points. You can rotate the chart, and you can pull out a slice by dragging it away from the pie. The individual slice can be formatted to make it stand out from the rest of the chart.

Do it!

A-2: Formatting a data point

Here's how	Here's why
1 Click the **Datapoint** sheet	This worksheet contains the total yearly bonus sales report for several products. The pie chart represents a breakdown of sales by product.
2 Select the slice representing cinnamon sales	(Click the pie and then click the largest slice.) You'll add a label to this data point using the Chart Elements button.
3 Click ⊞	(The Chart Elements button is to the right of the chart.) To open the Chart Elements menu.
In the Chart Elements menu, point to **Data Labels** and click the arrow as shown	**CHART ELEMENTS** ☐ Chart Title ☐ Data Labels ▸ ☑ Legend To open a submenu.
From the submenu, choose **More Options...**	To open the Format Data Label task pane.
4 Click as shown	Label Options To display the Label Options pane.
5 Under Label Contains, clear **Value**	You'll label the slice representing cinnamon sales as a percentage of the total.
Under Label Contains, check **Percentage**	
Under Label Position, select **Outside End**	To place the data label just outside the slice.
6 Expand **Number**	
From the Category list, select **Percentage**	To format the number as a percentage.
Edit the Decimal places box to read **0**	If necessary.
Close the Format Data Label task pane	To add the label.

7 Observe the chart

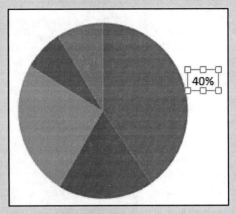

The new data label, representing the total value of cinnamon sales, appears outside the pie slice.

8 Click anywhere in the chart

To deselect the slice and data label.

Point to the cinnamon slice

A ScreenTip appears, showing the total value of cinnamon sales and the percentage of total product sales it represents.

9 Select the slice representing cinnamon sales

You'll make other changes to the slice.

10 Click the **Format** tab

Under Chart Tools, on the ribbon.

11 In the Current Selection group, click **Format Selection**

To open the Format Data Point dialog box. Series Options is selected by default.

12 Set the "Angle of first slice" value to **195**

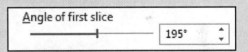

(Drag the slider or type the value in the box.) To rotate the pie chart so that the cinnamon slice occupies a 9 o'clock position.

Set the Point Explosion value to approximately **20%**

To pull out the slice representing cinnamon sales so that it is separate from the rest of the pie chart and the data point stands out from the others.

13 Click as shown

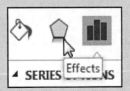

To open the Effects pane.

14 In the Effects list, expand
3-D Format

You'll give the slice some depth.

Click the arrow on the Top Bevel
button, as shown

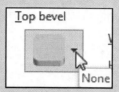

To open a gallery of bevel effects.

Select the indicated bevel option

To create the effect of a raised circle.

15 Close the Format Data Point task
pane

Deselect the slice

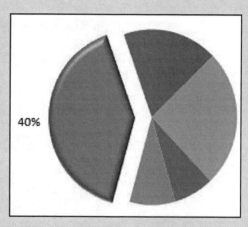

The slice now has a beveled edge to make it
even more distinct from the other slices.

16 Update and close the workbook

Topic B: Combination charts

Changing chart types and adding axes

Explanation

You can combine two or more chart types in a single chart, called a *combination chart*. For example, you can combine a column chart with a line chart. Other chart combinations are also possible. You can use combination charts when you want to represent a wider range of information or when you want to highlight a series or the contrast between series. You can also graphically represent variations in data by using trendlines and sparklines.

At times, you might need to show two kinds of information on the same chart. For example, in Exhibit 4-3, the columns show expense and sales figures, measured in thousands of dollars, while the line shows profit figures, which are percentages. You can create combination charts by applying a secondary axis to one or more data series. You can also change the chart type for that data series to make it stand out from the rest of the chart. This is especially useful if the values for that data series are very different from the values for the other data series.

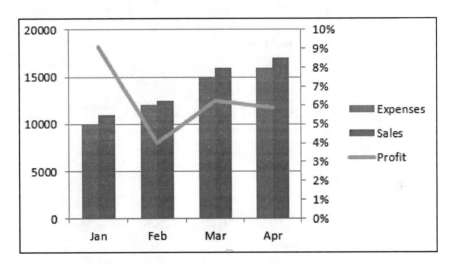

Exhibit 4-3: A sample column-line combination chart

To create a combination chart by changing the chart type of a data series:

1 Select the chart to display the Chart Tools tabs.

2 Click the Format tab.

3 In the Current Selection group, in the Chart Area list, select the data series for which you want to change the chart type.

4 Click Format Selection, and select formatting options.

5 Click the Design tab.

6 In the Type group, click Change Chart Type to open the Change Chart Type dialog box.

7 Select the chart type you want to apply to the selected data series.

8 Click OK.

To create a combination chart that uses a secondary value axis:

1 Select the chart and click the Format tab.

2 In the Current Selection group, in the Chart Area list, select the data series that will use the secondary value axis.

3 In the Current Selection group, click Format Selection to open the Format Data Series dialog box.

4 Under Plot Series On, select Secondary Axis.

5 Click Close.

Do it!

B-1: Creating a combination chart

The files for this activity are in Student Data folder **Unit 4\Topic B**.

Here's how	Here's why
1 Open Profit trends.xlsx	From the current topic folder.
Save the workbook as **My Profit trends.xlsx**	
Verify that **Combination** is the active sheet	This sheet displays profit trends for four months.
2 Observe the chart	

The category axis represents the months, and the value axis represents the sales. Profit columns are not visible because the Profit values are too small relative to the Expenses and Sales values.

3 Select the chart

4 Click the **Format** tab

5 In the Current Selection group, from the Chart Area list, select **Series "Profit"** as shown

You'll create a secondary value axis to represent the Profit data series.

6 Click **Format Selection**

To open the Format Data Series task pane. Series Options is selected by default.

7 Under Plot Series On, select **Secondary Axis**

To insert a secondary axis on the right side of the chart.

Close the task pane

The secondary axis appears on the right side of the chart. The chart columns for the Profit data series overlap the other columns.

8 Click the **Design** tab

9 In the Type group, click **Change Chart Type**

To open the Change Chart Type dialog box. You'll assign a separate chart type to the Profit data series so that it will be represented as a line.

Click the Recommended Charts tab

Excel will recommend a combination chart type based on the values in the chart and the formatting options you've chosen.

10 Observe the first recommended chart type

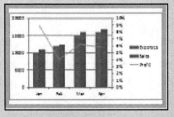

The combination chart type is "Clustered Column – Line on Secondary Axis."

Click **OK**

(You don't need to select the chart type, as it's already selected.) To close the gallery and change the chart type for the Profit data series from column to line, as shown in Exhibit 4-3. Now it's easier to understand how profit percentages fluctuate with respect to expenses and sales.

11 Update the workbook

Adding trendlines

Explanation

You can create a trendline in a chart to emphasize the pattern of change in your data. *Trendlines* are graphical representations of drifts or variations in a data series. Trendlines can highlight important variations, as shown in Exhibit 4-4, and make your charts easier to understand, and they can facilitate forecasting and decision making.

To add a trendline to a chart:

1. Select the chart or data series to which you want to add a trendline.
2. Click the Chart Elements button.
3. From the Trendlines style list, choose a trendline style.

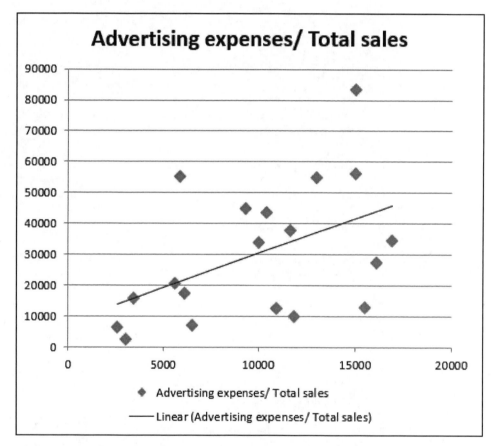

Exhibit 4-4: A chart with a linear trendline added

Do it!

B-2:   Adding a trendline

Here's how	Here's why
1 Click the **Trendline** sheet	It shows the advertising expenses and total sales for several years. In the chart, it's difficult to determine whether sales increased or decreased relative to changes in advertising expenses.
2 Select the chart	You'll create a trendline for the Advertising Expenses/Total Sales data series.
3 Click ✚	(The Chart Elements button to the right of the chart.) To open the list of chart elements.
Click the arrow next to **Trendline**	To display a menu of trendline style options.
Choose **Linear**	To apply a linear trendline to the chart. Your worksheet should look like Exhibit 4-4.
4 Deselect the chart, and update the workbook	

Sparklines

Explanation

In Excel, you can add sparklines to worksheets. A *sparkline* is a small chart that is inserted into a single cell to illustrate a pattern or trend in data. There are three types of sparklines: line, column, and win/loss. A sparkline chart resides in the background of a cell, so you can enter text on top of it.

Inserting sparkline

Sparklines can be inserted anywhere in a worksheet. However, it's recommended that they be adjacent to the data they are representing.

To insert a sparkline:

1   Select the cell(s) where you want to insert the sparkline.
2   Click the Insert tab.
3   In the Sparklines group, click the desired Sparkline button (Line, Column, or Win/Loss) to open the Create Sparklines dialog box, shown in Exhibit 4-5.
4   In the Data Range box, enter the range to be charted. Use the Collapse dialog box button, if necessary. **Note:** You can select multiple rows of data to create multiple sparklines at once.
5   In the Location Range box, verify that the destination is correct.
6   Click OK.

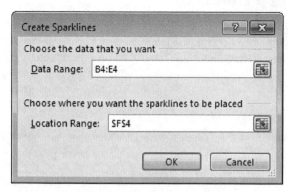

Exhibit 4-5: The Create Sparklines dialog box

Modifying sparklines

To modify a sparkline chart, use the buttons on the Sparkline Tools | Design tab. As with any other Excel chart, you can modify a sparkline by changing its type, applying a different style, changing the color or line weight, or showing data points and markers.

Product	Qtr1	Qtr2	Qtr3	Qtr4	Trend	Total sales
Cinnamon	$6,291	$5,209	$6,333	$8,633	Up	$26,466
Mustard seed	$791	$278	$298	$478		$11,845
Basil leaf	$432	$322	$245	$754		$16,500
Angelica root	$6,354	$6,563	$4,333	$8,284		$5,000
Anise	$789	$434	$564	$633		$5,700

Exhibit 4-6: Inserting sparklines in a worksheet

Do it!

B-3:   Inserting sparklines

Here's how	Here's why
1 Click the **Sales** sheet	You'll create sparklines that provide a visual representation of the sales figures.
2 Insert a column between columns E and F	
3 In F3, enter **Trend**	To give the new column a heading.
4 Select F4	(If necessary.) You can insert sparklines anywhere in the worksheet; however, it's recommended that you keep them adjacent to the data they depict.
Click the **Insert** tab	The Sparklines group provides three types of sparklines: Line, Column, and Win/Loss. The type you use depends on what you are trying to illustrate.
In the Sparklines group, click **Line**	To open the Create Sparklines dialog box.
5 In the Data Range box, enter **B4:E4**	If necessary, collapse the dialog box to select the range in the worksheet. You can also type directly in the Data Range box.
6 In the Location Range box, verify that F4 is specified	By default, the location is entered as an absolute reference.
Click **OK**	To close the dialog box and create a sparkline in cell F4. The sparkline chart illustrates the upward trend of cinnamon sales from the first to the last quarter.
7 Select F4	If necessary.
Drag to fill the sparkline down to F8	To insert sparklines in the range.

8	Select F4 and observe the formula bar	The formula bar is empty, because sparklines reside in the background of the cell
	In cell F4, enter **Up**	
		To enter text in the cell and see that it appears on top of the sparkline.
9	Select F4:F8	(If necessary.) As shown in Exhibit 4-6, the Sparkline Tools | Design tab is activated. As with other Excel charts, you can change the style and appearance of sparklines.
	In the Style gallery, explore the various styles	You can change the style of the sparkline, if you wish.
10	In the Type group, click **Column**	To change the sparkline chart type to Column.
	Click **Win/Loss**	To change the type to Win/Loss.
	Change the sparkline chart type back to **Line**	In the Type group, click Line.
11	In the Show group, check **High Point**	A marker is added to the highest point in each sparkline. You can add markers for the highest, lowest, first, last, or negative point or for all individual points. Use the Marker Color menu to change the marker colors.
12	Deselect the sparklines	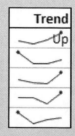
		You can clearly see the new sparklines with the highest-point markers, as shown in Exhibit 4-6.
13	Update the workbook	

Create a custom chart template

Explanation   You can save a formatted chart as a template. To do so, right-click the chart and choose Save as Template from the shortcut menu. In the Save Chart Template dialog box, shown in Exhibit 4-7, enter a file name. Click Save. By default, the new template will be saved in the Templates/Chart folder and will be available like other Excel charts.

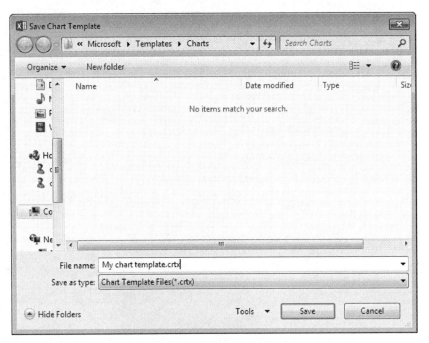

Exhibit 4-7: The Save Chart Template dialog box

Product	Qtr1	Qtr2	Qtr3	Qtr4	Total sales
Angelica Root	$6,291	$5,209	$6,333	$8,633	$22,703
Mustard seed	$791	$278	$298	$478	$11,845
Basil leaf	$432	$322	$245	$754	$16,500
Celery Seed	$6,354	$6,563	$4,333	$8,284	$6,200
Chives	$789	$434	$564	$633	$5,300

36%

- Angelica Root
- Mustard seed
- Basil leaf
- Celery Seed
- Chives

Exhibit 4-8: A worksheet with a custom chart template

Do it!

B-4: Creating and using a custom chart template

The files for this activity are in Student Data folder **Unit 4\Topic B**.

Here's how	Here's why
1 On the Sales sheet, right-click the chart	To open a shortcut menu.
2 Choose **Save as Template…**	To open the Save Chart Template dialog box. The chart template will be saved in the Templates/Charts folder, with the extension .crtx.
3 In the File name box, enter **My chart template**	
4 Click **Save**	To save the template and close the dialog box.
5 Click the Product sales sheet	You'll use the custom chart template in this sheet.
6 Select A4:A8 and F4:F8	This is the data on which the chart will be based.
Open the Insert Chart dialog box	Click the dialog box launcher in the Charts group on the Insert tab.
7 Activate the All Charts tab	
In the Chart Type list, select **Templates**	To open the Templates folder. My chart template is selected because it's the only template in the folder.
Click **OK**	To insert the template and close the dialog box. The pie chart reflects the selected data.
8 Position the chart so that the cell data is visible	Angelica Root is the biggest seller at 36% of total sales, as shown in Exhibit 4-8.
Update and close the workbook	

Topic C: Graphical objects

Drawing objects

Explanation

You can highlight a specific portion of a chart by adding graphical objects, such as text boxes, lines, and arrows. You can also format these objects, using special effects, or borders, to make them stand out or fit in better.

When you create or work with a shape, the Drawing Tools appear, adding a Format tab to the ribbon.

You can use the Shapes gallery to insert lines, arrows, text boxes, and other shapes in the chart area. To add a shape to a chart:

1 Select the chart and click the Format tab.

2 In the Insert Shapes group, open the Shapes gallery.

3 Select the desired shape and drag within the chart to create that shape.

Do it!

C-1: Adding graphical objects to charts

The files for this activity are in Student Data folder **Unit 4\Topic C**.

Here's how	Here's why
1 Open Revenue comparison.xlsx	
Save the workbook as **My revenue comparison.xlsx**	
2 Select the chart	You'll add some graphical objects to the chart.
Click the Format tab	
3 In the Insert Shapes group, click as shown	To insert a text box into the chart.
Drag to create a text box outside the chart	The Drawing Tools | Format tab appears on the ribbon. You'll move and resize the box.

4 Move the text box as shown

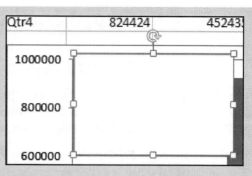

Drag it onto the chart.

5 Click in the text box and type **Sales hike**

You'll emphasize the steep rise in sales in the third quarter.

6 Resize the box to better fit the text

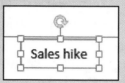

7 Select the text

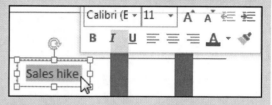

To open the Mini toolbar. You can change the font, font size, typestyle, and colors here.

   Apply the italic style to the text

8 Click the Format tab

Under Drawing Tools, on the ribbon.

9 In the Shapes gallery, click as shown

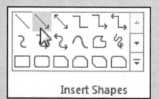

To select the Arrow line. The pointer takes the shape of a crosshair that you can use to draw an arrow.

10	Point to the upper-right corner of the text in the text box	The foot of the arrow will be here.
	Drag as shown	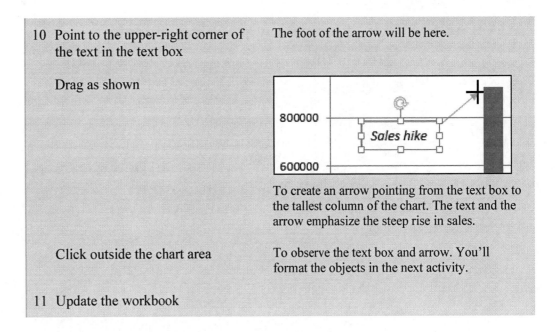
		To create an arrow pointing from the text box to the tallest column of the chart. The text and the arrow emphasize the steep rise in sales.
	Click outside the chart area	To observe the text box and arrow. You'll format the objects in the next activity.
11	Update the workbook	

Format graphical objects

Explanation

You can change the shape, size, outline, or color of graphical objects. Here's how:

1. Click the graphical object you want to format.
2. On the Format tab, in the Shape Styles group, click either the Shape Fill, Shape Outline, or Shape Effects button to display a corresponding menu.
3. Choose an option from the menu. Some menu options display galleries, as shown in Exhibit 4-9.

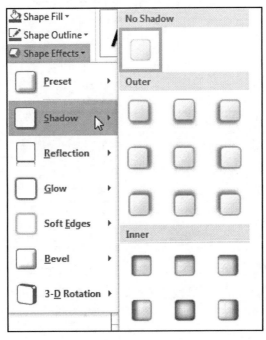

Exhibit 4-9: The Shadow gallery accessed from the Shape Effects menu

Do it!   ## C-2:   Formatting graphical objects

Here's how	Here's why
1 Click the Sales hike arrow	
Activate the Drawing Tools | Format tab	
2 In the Shape Styles group, click **Shape Effects** and open the Shadow gallery	As shown in Exhibit 4-9.
Point to the various effect options	To see a Live Preview of the effects.
Click anywhere outside the Shadow gallery	To close it.
3 In the Shape Styles group, click **Shape Outline**	To display shape options.
Point to **Arrows**	To display the Arrows gallery. The current arrowhead style is highlighted.
Click as shown	
	To apply Arrow Style 9 to the arrow in the chart.
4 Display the shape outline options again	Click Shape Outline.
In Theme Colors, choose the color indicated	
	To change the arrow's color to Red, Accent 2.
5 Apply an automatic border around the text box	Select the text box, then open the Shape Outline menu and choose Automatic.
6 Click outside the chart	To see the formatting changes you made.
Update and close the workbook	

Unit summary: Advanced charting

Topic A   In this topic, you adjusted the **scale** of a chart and formatted data points. You added **data labels**, such as the percentage value of a data point, to a chart. You also exploded a slice in a pie chart.

Topic B   In this topic, you created a **combination chart** by using two value axes. You also added **trendlines**, which can be used to highlight the variations of data in a data series. Finally, you created **sparklines** to illustrate trends or patterns.

Topic C   In this topic, you inserted **graphical objects** into a chart, and then you formatted the objects.

Review questions

1 How can you change the scale of a chart?

2 What is a leader line?

3 What is a combination chart?

4 What is a trendline?

5 Which of the following best describes a sparkline?

   A A graphical representation of trends in data

   B A small chart in a single cell that shows patterns in data

   C An animated SmartArt graphic

   D A line connecting data labels to their respective data points

Independent practice activity

In this activity, you'll change the values on the horizontal axis, change the maximum scale of the value axis, add a text box and arrow, and add a linear trendline.

The files for this activity are in Student Data folder **Unit 4\Unit summary**.

1 Open Practice charts.xlsx and save it as **My Practice charts.xlsx**.

2 Click the Bonus sales worksheet, if necessary.

3 Change the category (horizontal) axis values to read **Q1**, **Q2**, **Q3**, **Q4**. (*Hint:* The values are in column A of the data.)

4 Change the maximum scale value of the value axis to **250**.

5 Add a text box to the chart, and enter **Lowest sales** in the box. Resize the box and the text to fit, apply the bold style and an automatic border, then position the text box as shown in Exhibit 4-10.

6 Add an arrow leading from the text box to the column showing the lowest sales. Apply the Offset Left shadow effect to the arrow.

7 Compare your chart with Exhibit 4-10.

8 Create a linear trendline for the data in the Trends worksheet.

9 Update and close the workbook.

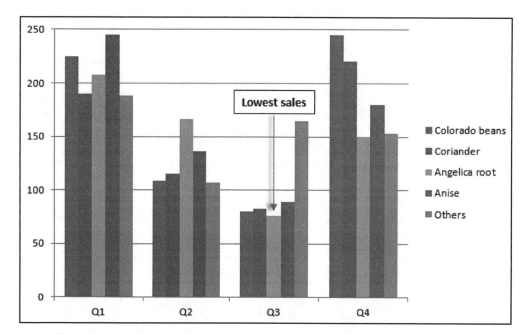

Exhibit 4-10: The chart after Step 6

Unit 5

PivotTables and PivotCharts

Complete this unit, and you'll know how to:

A Use the PivotTable command to create a PivotTable for analyzing and comparing large amounts of data.

B Change PivotTable views by grouping data, moving fields, and using calculated fields.

C Improve the appearance of a PivotTable by applying a style and changing its field settings.

D Create a PivotChart to graphically display data from a PivotTable.

Topic A: Working with PivotTables

Examining PivotTables

Explanation

By analyzing data, you can make more informed decisions. Excel provides the PivotTable feature to help you examine data. A *PivotTable* is an interactive table that summarizes, organizes, and compares large amounts of data in a worksheet. You can rotate the rows and columns in a PivotTable to obtain different views of the same data. You can use a PivotTable to analyze data in an Excel workbook or data from an external database, such as Microsoft Access or SQL Server.

The data on which a PivotTable is based is called the *source data*. Each column represents a *field*, or category of information, which you can assign to different parts of the PivotTable to determine how the data is arranged. You can add four types of fields, shown in Exhibit 5-1 and explained in the following table:

Field	Description
Filters	Filters the summarized data in the PivotTable. If you select an item in the report filter, the view of the PivotTable changes to display only the summarized data associated with that item. For example, if Region is a report filter, you can display the summarized data for the North region, the West region, or all regions.
Rows	Displays the items in a field as row labels. For example, in Exhibit 5-1, the row labels are values in the Quarter field, which means that the table shows one row for each quarter.
Columns	Displays the items in a field as column labels. For example, in Exhibit 5-1, the column labels are values in the Product field, which means that the table shows one column for each product.
Σ Values	Contains the summarized data. These fields usually contain numeric data, such as sales and inventory figures. The area where the data itself appears is called the *data area*.

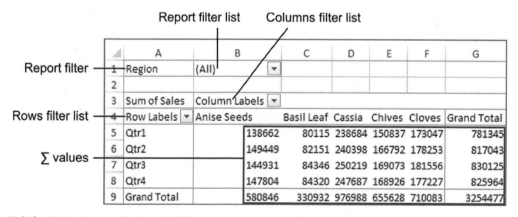

Exhibit 5-1: A sample PivotTable

The PivotTable command

You use the PivotTable command to create a PivotTable. Here's how:

1 Select any cell in a data range that includes a heading for each column in the top row.

2 Click the Insert tab.

3 In the Tables group, click the PivotTable button to open the Create PivotTable dialog box, shown in Exhibit 5-2.

4 In the Table/Range box, select the range that contains the data you want to use in the PivotTable.

5 Select a location for the PivotTable. You can place the PivotTable in a new or existing worksheet.

6 Click OK.

When you insert or work with PivotTables, Excel displays the PivotTable Tools, adding Analyze and Design tabs to the ribbon.

Exhibit 5-2: The Create PivotTable dialog box

Using an external data source

You can use an external data source as the data for the PivotTable. To do so:

1 In an empty worksheet, click the Insert tab and click the PivotTables button.

2 In the Create PivotTables dialog box, select "Use an external data source" and click Choose Connection.

3 From the list of connections, select the desired connection, such as an Access database. If the connection you want is not showing, click Browse for More.

4 Click Open. The selected data source appears as the Connection name.

5 Click OK to continue creating the PivotTable.

Do it!

A-1:   Creating a PivotTable

The files for this activity are in Student Data folder **Unit 5\Topic A**.

Here's how	Here's why
1 Open Sales analysis.xlsx	The Sales Data worksheet contains the sales and customer details for several products. You'll use the data in this worksheet to create a PivotTable.
2 Save the workbook as **My Sales analysis.xlsx**	In the current topic folder.
3 Select any cell in the data range	You'll create a PivotTable based on this range. If you select a cell within the range of the source data, you won't have to specify the range later.
4 Click the **Insert** tab	
5 In the Tables group, click **PivotTable**	To open the Create PivotTable dialog box. It prompts you to select the location of the data you want to analyze. You can use an external data source or an Excel worksheet. The default is the range that Excel automatically determines from the selected cell, as shown in Exhibit 5-2.
	You can create the PivotTable in a new or existing worksheet. The default selection is New Worksheet.
Click **OK**	A new worksheet, Sheet1, is added to the workbook. This worksheet displays the layout of the PivotTable. The PivotTable Fields task pane appears, and the PivotTable Tools	Analyze and Design tabs appear on the ribbon.
6 Edit the Sheet1 tab name to read **PivotTable**	Double-click the name, type the new one, and press Enter.
7 Update the workbook	

Add fields

Explanation

You add fields to a PivotTable to specify the data you want to display. The fields of the source data appear in the PivotTable Field List pane, shown in Exhibit 5-3.

To add fields, drag a field from the top of the PivotTable Fields task pane to one of the four areas at the bottom of the pane, as shown in Exhibit 5-3. You can add more than one field to an area, and you don't need to add all fields to the table. To display data and not just headings, you need to place at least one field in the Σ Values area.

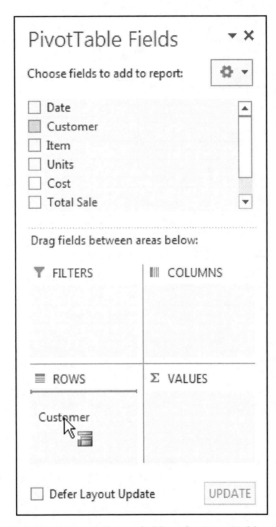

Exhibit 5-3: Adding a field to the PivotTable

Using fields to filter data

After the fields are in place, you can filter the information that appears in the table by selecting options from the filter lists available for each field. For example, you can show all data values or restrict the PivotTable to summarizing only a couple of values.

When a filter has been applied, the arrow changes to a filter icon (it looks like a funnel). You can click this icon to display the filter list and see which filter has been applied.

To remove a filter, display the filter list and choose the Clear Filter option. You can also display the filter list by clicking the corresponding filter icon in the PivotTable Field List pane.

Do it!   ## A-2:   Adding fields to a PivotTable

Here's how	Here's why
1 Verify that the PivotTable sheet is active	You'll add fields in the PivotTable layout.
Observe the PivotTable Fields task pane	(The entire pane is shown in Exhibit 5-3.) It displays the column headings of the source data in the PivotTable worksheet.
2 Point to **Customer**	The pointer turns into a four-headed arrow. You'll place this field in the Rows area.
Drag **Customer** to the Rows area, as shown	≣ ROWS Customer In the PivotTable Fields pane.
3 Observe the worksheet	Row Labels ▾ Accounts Now Award Sportswear Blastera BlazerFire Brocadero The customer names are now row labels, and the list can be filtered.
4 In the pane, drag **Item** to the Columns area	To add Item as a column heading field.
5 Drag **Total Sale** to the Σ Values area	To add Total Sale as the Σ Values field. The PivotTable shows the sum of total sales of items per customer.
6 In the worksheet, click as shown	Column Labels ▾ Cogs To display a drop-down menu that includes an Item list.
Clear **Select All**	
Check **Gadgets**	To filter the list so that only the sales information for the Gadgets item is shown.
Click **OK**	The worksheet now shows the sales figures for only Gadgets. At the right end of Column Labels, the funnel icon indicates that a filter has been applied.

7	Click the arrow for **Row Labels**	To display the list of customers.
	Filter the list so that only the information for BlazerFire will be displayed	Clear Select All, check BlazerFire, and click OK. The PivotTable data is now filtered to show only the Gadget sales for BlazerFire.
8	Clear the filters from the Item and Customer fields	(Click the arrows for both fields and choose Clear File from "<fieldname>".) To display all items and customers.
9	Update the workbook	

Inserting slicers

Explanation

As shown in Exhibit 5-4, the filter icon in cell B1 indicates that the PivotTable is displaying the sales figures for only the Central region. However, when you apply more than one filter, the filter is often labeled as "Multiple items." This designation is not particularly helpful. In Excel, you can insert a slicer to easily show the current filtered state of the data. You can create a slicer for each field in the PivotTable.

Slicers are visual controls you can use to quickly filter your data by selecting values from a list. Slicers are both "live"—they reflect data changes in the underlying PivotTable—and interactive—you can select filter fields on the fly. Slicers appear as separate objects on the worksheet and can be moved around and resized.

To insert a slicer:

1 Select any cell in the PivotTable.
2 Click the PivotTable Tools | Analyze tab. In the Filter group, click Insert Slicer. The Insert Slicers dialog box appears with a list of the PivotTable fields.
3 Check the fields you want to display as slicers.
4 Click OK. The slicers appear on top of the PivotTable, and the Slicer Tools | Options tab appears on the ribbon.

Using slicers to filter data

Even though the slicers are overlapping, it's possible to see which filters are selected, as shown in Exhibit 5-4. The selected items on the slicer indicate which filter is being applied. On the Region slicer, Central is the only highlighted item. The Product slicer indicates that no filter is applied because all items are selected (or highlighted).

To change a slicer filter, click the item you want to use as the filter. Use the Ctrl+click method to select multiple items. Use the Shift+click method to select contiguous items. To clear the filter, click the Clear Filter button at the right end of the slicer header.

Modifying slicers

Excel considers slicers to be shapes. Therefore, you can move, resize, align, and format slicers just as you would other shapes. To move a slicer, drag the slicer header to the desired location. Drag a slicer's border to change the size of the slicer. Use the Slicer Tools | Options tab to apply a slicer style and to align the slicers.

Deleting slicers

You can quickly delete a slicer by selecting it and pressing Delete. You can also right-click the slicer and choose Remove "*Slicer Name*" from the shortcut menu. The slicer is immediately removed.

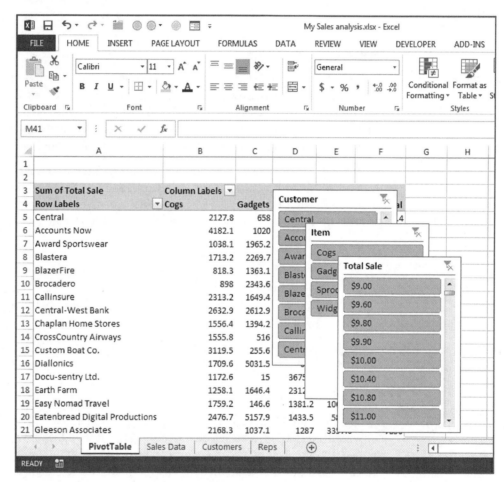

Exhibit 5-4: The PivotTable with slicers

Do it!

A-3:   Using slicers to filter PivotTable data

Here's how	Here's why
1 On the Analyze tab, in the Filter group, click **Insert Slicer**	The Insert Slicers dialog box opens.
2 Check **Customer**, **Item**, and **Total Sale**	To create slicers for the Customer, Item, and Total Sale fields.
3 Click **OK**	As shown in Exhibit 5-4, the three slicers appear overlapped.
4 Using the slicer headers, drag the slicers so they do not overlap	You can move slicers anywhere on the worksheet. They can even be moved or copied to a separate worksheet. Notice that the Slicer Tools | Options tab has appeared on the ribbon.
5 On the Customer slice, click **Award Sportswear**, as shown	Customer Central Accounts Now Award Sportswear Blastera To display only the Award Sportwear data.
Press ⌈CTRL⌋ and click **Central**	To add Central to the Customer filter.
6 On the Item slicer, click **Cogs**	To display only the Cog sales figures for the Central and Award Sportswear customers.
Press ⌈SHIFT⌋ and click **Widgets**	Item Cogs Gadgets Sprockets Widgets To select Gadgets, Sprockets, and Widgets.

7 On the Options tab, click **Selection Pane**

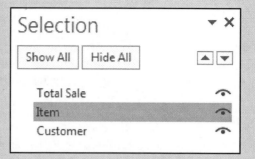

To open the Selection pane. The eye icons indicate which slicers are visible. You can click the icon to show or hide the respective slicer.

8 Click **Hide All**

To hide all slicers.

Click **Show All**

To show all slicers again. The PivotTable Fields pane might also appear.

9 For the Item slicer, click 👁

The slicer remains listed in the Selection and Visibility pane, but the "closed eye" indicates that the slicer is hidden.

10 Observe the Customer and Total Sale slicers

When slicers contain a lengthy list of items, you can use the scrollbar to view the additional items.

Right-click the header of the Total Sale slicer and choose **Remove "Total Sale"**

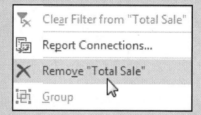

To delete the slicer from the worksheet. It no longer appears in the Selection and Visibility pane.

11 Update and close the workbook

Topic B: Modifying PivotTable data

Group data

Explanation

You may have certain data in your PivotTable that needs to be further summarized. You can do this by grouping the data.

You can group text fields, number fields, and date fields. To group data:

1 Select a row or column cell containing the type of data you want to group.
2 On the Analyze tab, click Group, and select a grouping option. Alternatively, you can right-click the cell and choose Group from the shortcut menu.
3 In the Grouping dialog box, enter the Starting at: and Ending at: values, and enter or select a By: value.
4 Click OK.

Move fields

Explanation

After creating a PivotTable, you might want to display an entirely different view of the data. You can change the data view by dragging the fields to other areas in the PivotTable. The PivotTable provides options to show or hide the details. To change data in the PivotTable, however, you need to refresh the table after changing the source data.

You can move a field in a PivotTable by dragging the field to a new area in the PivotTable Field List pane. To show a columnar view of the data, as shown in Exhibit 5-5, drag a report or row field to the Column Labels box in the pane. When you want to arrange data in row fields, drag a report or column field to the Row Labels box in the pane.

Sum of Total Sale	Column Labels				
Row Labels	Qtr1	Qtr2	Qtr3	Qtr4	Grand Total
Cogs	21098.8	19641	17983.6	15262.2	73985.6
Gadgets	18926.7	15469.8	16689.6	25765.5	76851.6
Sprockets	13962	22503.2	17686.2	16694.7	70846.1
Widgets	21151.7	22911.8	17487	15112.3	76662.8
Grand Total	75139.2	80525.8	69846.4	72834.7	298346.1

Exhibit 5-5: A PivotTable with fields rearranged and records grouped by date

Do it!

B-1: Grouping data and moving fields

The files for this activity are in Student Data folder **Unit 5\Topic B**.

Here's how	Here's why
1 Open Sales analysis2.xlsx	
Save it as **My Sales analysis2.xlsx**	In the current topic folder.
Observe the PivotTable	It shows the sales of several products, by customer. You'll rearrange the fields, add the date field, and group the date records.
2 In the PivotTable Fields task pane, click as shown	▤ ROWS Customer ⟍ To open a shortcut menu.
From the shortcut menu, choose **Remove Field**	To remove the Customer field from the PivotTable layout. You want to view only the item sales totals.
3 Drag **Item** to the Rows area	Each item is now a row label in the PivotTable.
4 Drag **Date** to the Columns area	To add the Date field to the PivotTable.
Observe the PivotTable	The dates are listed individually as column labels, extending out of view. You want to summarize sales data more meaningfully by grouping the date records.
5 Select one of the dates	
6 On the Analyze tab, click **Group**	To open the Group menu.
Choose **Group Field**	→ Group Selection ▦ Ungroup 🗓 Group Field ⟍ Group To open the Grouping dialog box.
7 In the dialog box, click **Months**	To deselect it.
Click **Quarters**	To group the dates by quarters.
Click **OK**	To close the dialog box and perform the grouping.

8 Observe the PivotTable again	The data is now organized so that quarterly sales totals for the items are displayed, as shown in Exhibit 5-5.
9 Update the workbook	

Refreshing PivotTable data

Explanation

You cannot directly change the data in a PivotTable because it's based on source data. To change data in a PivotTable, you must first change the source data and then refresh the PivotTable to reflect the latest changes.

You can refresh the PivotTable by clicking the Refresh button in the Data group on the Analyze tab.

Do it!

B-2: Refreshing the data in a PivotTable

Here's how	Here's why
1 Select E6	It displays 25765.5, which is the value of the Qtr 4 sales of Gadgets.
Type **2**	 Microsoft Excel ⚠ Cannot change this part of a PivotTable report. [OK] Was this information helpful? When you try to enter a new value, a message box appears with a warning that you can't change the value in a PivotTable.
Click **OK**	To close the message box.
2 Click the Sales Data sheet	This sheet contains the source data for the PivotTable. To change the data in the PivotTable, you have to change the values in the source data.
3 Select D3	You'll change this value and then view the result in the PivotTable.
Edit D3 to read **300**	
4 Click the PivotTable sheet	Notice that E6 still shows the old value.
5 Click the Analyze tab	
6 In the Data group, click **Refresh**	(The top half of the Refresh button.) To update the PivotTable with the latest data. E6 now shows the adjusted value of 26045.5.
7 Update the workbook	

Insert calculated fields

Explanation

You can create new fields in a PivotTable that calculate values based on the data in other PivotTable fields. In other words, a calculated field will show the results of a formula, rather than the original values from the underlying source data. For example, you can create a Commission field with a formula that calculates a percentage of total sales as a commission value.

To insert a calculated field:

1. Select a cell in the PivotTable.
2. On the Analyze tab, in the Calculations group, click Fields, Items, & Sets.
3. Choose Calculated Field, to open the Insert Calculated Field dialog box.
4. Specify a name for the calculated field, and enter the formula you want to use.
5. Click Insert.

Do it!

B-3: Inserting a calculated field

The files for this activity are in Student Data folder **Unit 5\Topic B**.

Here's how	Here's why
1 Select a cell in the PivotTable	If necessary.
2 Remove the Total Sale field from the PivotTable layout	(Click the arrow on the field and choose Remove Field.) You'll replace this field with a new, calculated field.
3 In the Calculations group, click **Fields, Items, & Sets**	You'll insert a field that will calculate an estimation of profit on the Total Sale data.
Choose **Calculated Field...**, as shown	
	To open the Insert Calculated Field dialog box.
4 In the dialog box, in the Name box, type **Est. Profit**	
5 Edit the Formula box to read **=.2*'Total Sale'**	To calculate an estimated profit of 2% of total sales.
6 Click **OK**	To close the dialog box and insert the new field.
7 Observe the PivotTable	The field values all show the result of the formula, and the field Est.Profit has been added to the Σ Values area of the layout.
Update and close the workbook	

Topic C: Formatting PivotTables

Formatting PivotTable data

Explanation

You can change the format of a PivotTable by using styles and the Field Settings dialog box. You can use styles to format an entire PivotTable in one step. You can use the Field Settings dialog box to change number formats, specify how data is summarized, and show or hide data.

Using styles

To display formatting options that affect the entire PivotTable, click the PivotTable Tools | Design tab. Some of the styles are specifically designed for PivotTables. Exhibit 5-6 shows a sample PivotTable style.

Sum of Total Sale	Column Labels ▼				
Row Labels ▼	Cogs	Gadgets	Sprockets	Widgets	Grand Total
Central	2127.8	658	645.3	2388.3	5819.4
Accounts Now	4182.1	1020	861.5	856	6919.6
Award Sportswear	1038.1	1965.2	624.3	1566.9	5194.5
Blastera	1713.2	2269.7	1941	1674.2	7598.1
BlazerFire	818.3	1363.1	947.7	3184.5	6313.6

Exhibit 5-6: A sample PivotTable style

Do it!

C-1: Applying a PivotTable style

The files for this activity are in Student Data folder **Unit 5\Topic C**.

Here's how	Here's why
1 Open Sales analysis3.xlsx	
Save the workbook as **My Sales analysis3.xlsx**	In the current topic folder.
2 Select any cell within the PivotTable	To activate the PivotTable Tools tabs.
Click the **Design** tab	If necessary.
3 In the PivotTable Styles group, open the PivotTable Styles gallery	Click the More button.
4 Under Medium, select the indicated style	To apply Pivot Style Medium 2 to the PivotTable. The PivotTable appears as shown in Exhibit 5-6.
5 Update the workbook	

Change field settings

Explanation

You can change field settings to alter how data appears or is summarized in a PivotTable. To change field settings:

1 Select any cell in the data area.
2 Click the PivotTable Tools | Analyze tab.
3 In the Active Field group, click Field Settings to open the Value Field Settings dialog box, shown in Exhibit 5-7.
4 Click the Number Format button to open the Format Cells dialog box. Select the desired options and click OK.
5 Click OK.

Exhibit 5-7: The Value Field Settings dialog box

Do it!   **C-2:   Changing field settings**

Here's how	Here's why
1 Select B5	You'll apply a number format to the sales numbers.
2 Click the Analyze tab	
3 In the Active Field group, click **Field Settings**	To open the Value Field Settings dialog box, shown in Exhibit 5-7.
4 Click **Number Format**	To open the Format Cells dialog box, with the Number tab active.
From the Category list, select **Currency**	To display the formatting options under Currency. The $ option is selected in the Symbol list. You'll add this prefix symbol to the sales values.
Edit the Decimal places box to read **0**	

Category:

General	
Number	Sample
Currency	$21,099
Accounting	
Date	Decimal places: [0]
Time	Symbol: [$]
Percentage	

To specify that currency values should be displayed as whole-dollar amounts.

Click **OK**	To close the Format Cells dialog box.
5 Click **OK**	To close the Value Field Settings dialog box and apply the formatting to all Total Sale field values (not just the selected cell). The values are now formatted with commas and the $ symbol.
6 Update and close the workbook	

Topic D: Using PivotCharts

Creating PivotCharts

Explanation

You can use a PivotChart to graphically display data from a PivotTable. A single PivotChart provides different views of the same data.

When you create a PivotChart, the row fields of the PivotTable become the categories, and the column fields become the series.

To create a PivotChart, select any cell in a PivotTable and click PivotChart in the Tools group on the PivotTable Tools | Analyze tab. In the Insert Chart dialog box, select options as you would for a standard chart, and click OK.

You can also create a new PivotChart and PivotTable at the same time. To do so, you select a cell in the source data, click the Insert tab, click the PivotTable button's arrow (in the Charts group), and choose PivotChart & PivotTable.

Changing the view of a PivotChart

In Excel 2013, Microsoft improved the way you change the view of a PivotChart. As shown in Exhibit 5-8, PivotCharts contain field buttons that are used to change what is displayed for a specific field. For example, to change the regions shown in the sample PivotChart, click the Region field button and select the regions you want to show. The same method can be used to filter the Product and Quarter fields.

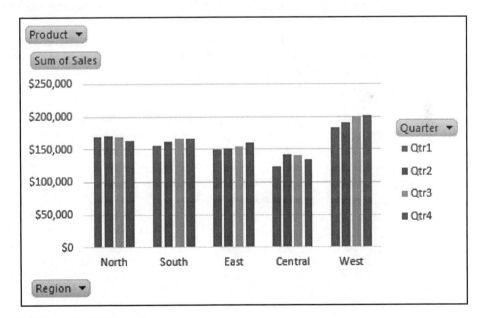

Exhibit 5-8: A PivotChart

PivotChart styles

As with PivotTables, you can apply built-in styles to your PivotChart. To do so:

1 Select the PivotChart.
2 On the Design tab, in the Chart Styles group, select the desired chart style.
3 Alternatively, click the Chart Styles button to the right of the selected chart, and choose a style from the gallery.

Do it!

D-1: Creating a PivotChart

The files for this activity are in Student Data folder **Unit 5\Topic D**.

Here's how	Here's why
1 Open Sales chart.xlsx	
Save the workbook as **My Sales chart.xlsx**	In the current topic folder.
Click anywhere within the PivotTable	(If necessary.) To indicate which data to use for the PivotChart.
2 Click the Analyze tab	
In the Tools group, click **PivotChart**	To open the Insert Chart dialog box. You'll create the default Column chart.
Click **OK**	To create a PivotChart in a floating box on this sheet. In the PivotChart Fields task pane, the field box titles reflect the Legend and Axis, and the boxes contain the active fields. The chart's X-axis displays the Rows fields; the legend displays the Columns; and the bars represent the data values. You'll change the PivotTable and chart to show only the total sales for each region.
3 In the PivotTable Fields task pane, drag **Product** to Filters	
	To make Product the report filter. You can now sort and filter data by product in the PivotChart.
Observe the PivotChart	As shown in Exhibit 5-8, the total sales for the five regions appear in columns, and each column is divided into quarters. You can use the Product, Region, and Quarter buttons to change the data displayed in the PivotChart.
Resize and move the chart so it does not overlap the table	

4 On the PivotChart, click
   Product, as indicated

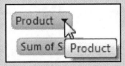

To display the Product items.

Select **Basil Leaf**   To show only the Basil Leaf data in the
                         PivotChart.

Click **OK**   The PivotChart displays the total sales of only
                Basil Leaf for all regions. The axis scale has
                adjusted to reflect the filtered figures.

5 From the Quarter list, clear all of
   the options except Qtr1

Click **OK**

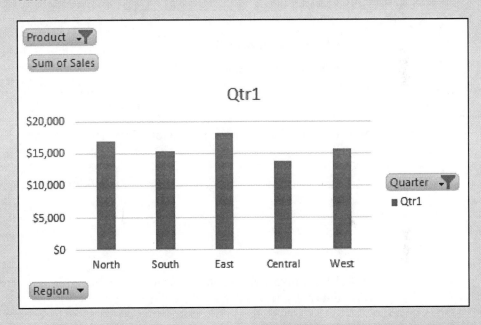

The chart displays the total sales of Basil Leaf in
the first quarter for all regions. The Product and
Quarter buttons contain icons indicating that the
chart data has been filtered.

6 With the PivotChart selected,   You'll apply a built-in chart style.
   click the Design tab

Select Style 4, as shown

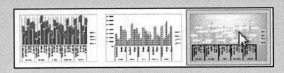

7 Update and close the workbook

Unit summary: PivotTables and PivotCharts

Topic A   In this topic, you learned that a **PivotTable** is used to summarize, organize, and compare large amounts of data in a worksheet. You created a PivotTable and added **fields** to the layout of a PivotTable. You also inserted **slicers** to filter the data.

Topic B   In this topic, grouped data in a PivotTable by a date field. Then, you changed the view of data in a PivotTable by moving the **row** and **column fields** to different areas. You changed a value in the source data and refreshed the PivotTable to reflect that change. Finally, you inserted a calculated field in the PivotTable.

Topic C   In this topic, you applied **styles** to format a PivotTable. You also used the Value Field Settings dialog box to apply formatting to numerical data.

Topic D   In this topic, you learned that a **PivotChart** graphically displays data from a PivotTable, and you created a PivotChart. You also used the **field buttons** to change which data is displayed for a specific field in a PivotChart. Finally, you applied a built-in style to the PivotChart.

Review questions

1   What is a PivotTable?

2   How do you start creating a PivotTable?

3   Can you directly change the data in a PivotTable? If not, how do you change the data?

4   Which PivotTable feature is used to easily identify the current filters applied to the data?

   A   Row labels

   B   PivotChart

   C   Slicers

   D   Field list

5   Why would you use a PivotChart?

6   How do you create a PivotChart?

Independent practice activity

In this activity, you'll create a PivotTable, modify it, and apply a style to it. Then you'll create and modify a PivotChart.

The files for this activity are in Student Data folder **Unit 5\Unit summary**.

1 Open Sales 2008-2012.

2 Save the workbook as **My Sales 2008-2012**.

3 Create a PivotTable based on the data in the Raw Data worksheet. (*Hint:* Select any cell in the data, and click the PivotTable button on the Insert tab.)

4 Move Year to the Rows area, move Quarter to the Columns area, move Product to the Rows area (below the Year field), and move Sales to the Σ Values area.

5 Apply the PivotTable Style Medium 3 style to the PivotTable. Compare your results with Exhibit 5-9.

6 Create a clustered column PivotChart.

7 Make **Quarter** and **Year** report filters in the PivotChart. (*Hint:* Drag the fields to Filters.)

8 Change the PivotChart to display the sales in the fourth quarter of 2012.

9 Compare your results with Exhibit 5-10.

10 Update and close the workbook.

Sum of Sales	Column Labels				
Row Labels	Qtr1	Qtr2	Qtr3	Qtr4	Grand Total
2008	**123443**	**141209**	**139751**	**134895**	**539298**
Anise Seeds	26000	33112	28874	27220	115206
Basil Leaf	13800	15080	12821	16363	58064
Cassia	45000	43983	46343	45892	181218
Chives	18300	25034	28679	25655	97668
Cloves	20343	24000	23034	19765	87142
2009	**139490.59**	**159566.17**	**157918.63**	**152431.35**	**609406.74**
Anise Seeds	29380	37416.56	32627.62	30758.6	130182.78
Basil Leaf	15594	17040.4	14487.73	18490.19	65612.32
Cassia	50850	49700.79	52367.59	51857.96	204776.34
Chives	20679	28288.42	32407.27	28990.15	110364.84
Cloves	22987.59	27120	26028.42	22334.45	98470.46
2010	**165413.62**	**189220.06**	**187266.34**	**180759.3**	**722659.32**
Anise Seeds	34840	44370.08	38691.16	36474.8	154376.04
Basil Leaf	18492	20207.2	17180.14	21926.42	77805.76
Cassia	60300	58937.22	62099.62	61495.28	242832.12
Chives	24522	33545.56	38429.86	34377.7	130875.12
Cloves	27259.62	32160	30865.56	26485.1	116770.28

Exhibit 5-9: The PivotTable after Step 5

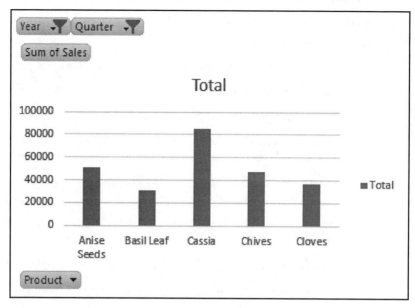

Exhibit 5-10: The PivotChart after Step 8

Unit 6

Exporting and importing data

Complete this unit, and you'll know how to:

A Export data from Excel to a text file, and import data from a text file into an Excel workbook.

B Use Microsoft Query and the Web query feature to import data from external databases.

Topic A: Exporting and importing text files

Sharing Excel data

Explanation

You can share information between Excel and other programs in a number of ways, including by using linked objects and copied data. Another way to share data is to export it from Excel to another format or to import data from another format into Excel. Excel can import from and export to files in several formats, including text files.

Using the Save As command to export data

You can use the Save As command to save an Excel workbook in a file format associated with the program in which you want to use the data. However, when you save an Excel workbook in a different file format, it might not retain its original formatting.

The following table describes some formats commonly used to export Excel data.

File format	Description
Text (tab delimited)	– Saves text and values as they appear in the worksheet
	– Saves formulas as text
	– Uses tab characters to separate columns of data
	– Uses paragraph marks to separate rows
	– Loses any formatting, graphics, and objects in the worksheet
	– Can be a useful way to fix a corrupted file
XML Paper Specification (XPS)	– Preserves formatting and graphics
	– Enables file sharing
	– Prevents data from being changed
	– XPS View is installed by default
Portable Document Format (PDF)	– Preserves formatting and graphics
	– Enables file sharing
	– Provides a standard format when using commercial printers
	– Abode Reader is freely available for download
Open Document Spreadsheet (ODS)	– Maintains some formatting, but not all
	– Opens in spreadsheet applications such as Google Docs

Do it!

A-1:   Exporting Excel data to a text file

The files for this activity are in Student Data folder **Unit 6\Topic A**.

Here's how	Here's why
1 Open Regional sales.xlsx	
2 Open the Save As dialog box	The File name box contains "Regional sales."
Edit the File name box to read **My Regional sales**	
From the Save as type list, select **Text (Tab delimited) (*.txt)**	This option will save the active sheet as a tab-delimited text file.
Click **Save**	To save the active sheet as a text file. A message appears, stating that Excel will not save those features that are not compatible with the Text (Tab delimited) file format.
Click **Yes**	To keep the tab-delimited format.
3 In Windows Explorer, navigate to the current topic folder	
Double-click **My Regional sales.txt**	To open the file in Notepad. The data from the Regional sales worksheet appears in the text file. All of the sales figures that contain commas appear in double quotation marks.
4 Switch to Excel	If necessary.
5 Close the workbook	You don't need to save changes.

Importing data

Explanation

By using the Open command in Excel, you can open a file created in a program other than Excel. After importing the data, you can save the file either in its original format or as an Excel workbook.

To import a file into an Excel workbook, you open the Open dialog box, specify the type of file you want to import, select the file, and click Open.

If you're importing a text file, Excel displays the Text Import Wizard, shown in Exhibit 6-1. The wizard guides you through the process of converting the text data into an Excel worksheet. As necessary, you can specify *delimiters* (the characters that determine when a new column should begin) and formatting for specific columns. After importing, you can separate text into columns, if necessary, by clicking Text to Columns in the Data Tools group on the Data tab.

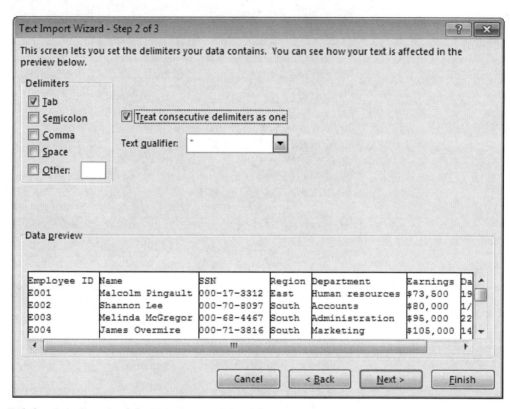

Exhibit 6-1: Step 2 of the Text Import Wizard

Do it!

A-2: Importing data from a text file into a workbook

The files for this activity are in Student Data folder **Unit 6\Topic A**.

Here's how	Here's why
1 Switch to Notepad	Click the Notepad taskbar button. The text file "My regional sales" is still open.
Open the Employee List text file	You'll import data from this text file into Excel. This file contains details for employees, with columns separated by tab characters.
Observe the date format in the last column	The person who entered this data used the European day/month/year format, not the American month/day/year format.
2 Close Notepad	
3 In Excel, display the Open dialog box	
Navigate to the current topic folder	
4 In the File type list, select **Text Files**, as shown	All Excel Files (*.xl*;*.xlsx;*.xlsm; ▼) All Files (*.*) All Excel Files (*.xl*;*.xlsx;*.xlsm;*.xls Excel Files (*.xl*;*.xlsx;*.xlsm;*.xlsb;*. All Web Pages (*.htm;*.html;*.mht; XML Files (*.xml) Text Files (*.prn;*.txt;*.csv) All Data Sources (*.odc;*.udl;*.dsn;* Access Databases (*.mdb;*.mde;*.a To display only the text files in the current topic folder.
Select **Employee list.txt**	To select the file you want to import.
5 Click **Open**	To open Step 1 of the Text Import Wizard. Under Original data type, Delimited is selected. The "Start import at row" box displays "1."
Click **Next**	In Step 2 of the Text Import Wizard, you can set the delimiter and see a preview of the data. Here, Tab is the default delimiter.
Under Data preview, observe the box	This box shows you how the data will look in Excel. Data in a few columns is misaligned with the headings because of the consecutive tabs.
Check **Treat consecutive delimiters as one**	To remove the blank columns, as shown in Exhibit 6-1.

6	Click **Next**	In Step 3 of the Text Import Wizard, you can specify the data format for each column.
7	Select the last column	(Scroll to the right as necessary.) You must indicate that the values are currently in DMY (day/month/year) format for Excel to be able to change the formatting to the American MDY format.
8	Under Column data format, select **Date**	
	From the Date format list, select **DMY**	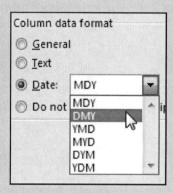
9	Click **Finish**	To close the Text Import Wizard. The worksheet shows the imported data. Some columns are too narrow to display all of the data.
10	Select columns A through G	
	Double-click the dividing line between any two selected column headings	To automatically fit the width to the column contents.
11	Observe the Date of Hire column data	Excel converted the dates to the MDY format.
12	Open the Save As dialog box	The File name box contains "Employee list.txt," and the Save as type list displays "Text (Tab delimited) (*.txt)"
	From the Save as type list, select **Excel Workbook (*.xlsx)**	(You might have to scroll up the list.) To save the data as an Excel workbook.
	Edit the File name box to read **My Employee list**	
13	Click **Save**	

Converting text to columns

Explanation

You can use the Text to Columns feature to divide text fields into two or more columns. This process works much like importing data from external text files. For instance, if you have one field for names, you can split this field into first-name and last-name columns. To do so, select the text field you want to convert and click Text to Columns on the Data tab. Follow the instructions in the Convert Text to Columns Wizard, shown in Exhibit 6-2.

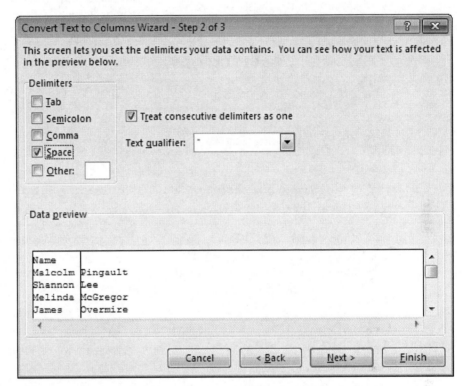

Exhibit 6-2: Step 2 of the Convert Text to Columns Wizard

Do it!   **A-3:   Converting text to columns**

Here's how	Here's why
1 Insert a column after column B	(Select column C, right-click it, and choose Insert.) To make room for the new column for storing last names.
2 Select column B	This is the Name column in the data you just imported from a text file.
3 On the Data tab, in the Data Tools group, click **Text to Columns**	To start the Convert Text to Columns Wizard. This is like a mini version of the Text Import Wizard.
4 Click **Next**	
5 Under Delimiters, clear **Tab** and check **Space**	As shown in Exhibit 6-2.
Check **Treat consecutive delimiters as one**	If necessary.
Click **Next**	To proceed to the last step in the wizard.
6 Verify that **General** is selected as the column data format	Note that the column heading Name appears in the first-name column. You'll change the heading after the conversion.
7 Click **Finish**	To close the wizard and return to the table. First and last names are now split into two columns. If you hadn't inserted a new column, Excel would have asked if you wanted to replace the existing data.
8 Edit B1 to read **First Name**	
9 In C1, enter **Last Name**	
10 Adjust column widths as necessary	
11 Update the workbook	

Removing duplicates

Explanation

Sometimes, especially when you import data from one or more external sources, you can end up with duplicate records. Using the Remove Duplicates dialog box, shown in Exhibit 6-3, you can remove duplicate records based on values in one or more fields. For instance, if you imported customer data from several sources because you want to compile e-mail addresses for a mailing, you can remove duplicates based on the E-mail field.

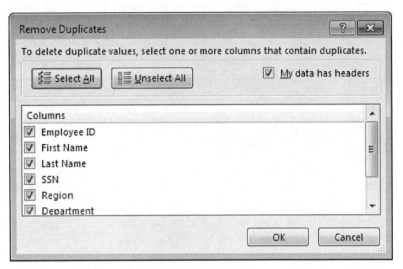

Exhibit 6-3: The Remove Duplicates dialog box

Do it!

A-4: Removing duplicate records

Here's how	Here's why
1 Observe employee numbers E005, E015, and E019	The table has duplicate records.
2 Select the table	
	Click the selector in the upper-left corner, as shown.
3 On the Data tab, in the Data Tools group, click **Remove Duplicates**	To open the Remove Duplicates dialog box.
4 Click **Unselect All**	You need to search only one column.
5 Check **SSN**	
	You'll search for duplicates based on the Social Security number, which should be a unique identifier.
6 Click **OK**	To close the Remove Duplicates dialog box. A message box informs you that three duplicates were found and removed.
Click **OK**	To close the message box.
7 Update and close the workbook	

Topic B: Getting external data

Explanation

With Microsoft Query, you can retrieve data from external databases, such as those in Microsoft Access. You can use the Web query feature to retrieve data from the Web.

Microsoft Query

You can use Microsoft Query to retrieve data that meets certain conditions in one or more tables of a database. For example, from an Employee table, you can retrieve the records of all people who work in the Marketing department.

To retrieve data by using Microsoft Query:

1   Click the Data tab.
2   In the Get External Data group, click From Other Sources and choose From Microsoft Query to start the Microsoft Query program and to open the Choose Data Source dialog box, shown in Exhibit 6-4.
3   On the Databases tab, select <New Data Source> and click OK to open the Create New Data Source dialog box. Specify the name of the data source and select a driver for the database. Click Connect to open the ODBC Microsoft Access Setup dialog box.
4   Under Database, click Select to open the Select Database dialog box. Select the source database, and then return to the Choose Data Source dialog box.
5   Select the data source, and click OK to open the Choose Columns page of the Query Wizard. Add the tables and fields you want to include in your result set. Click Next to open the Filter Data page of the Query Wizard.
6   Specify the conditions you want the data to meet. Click Next to open the Sort Order page of the Query Wizard.
7   Specify the sort order for the data. Click Next to open the Finish page of the Query Wizard.
8   Select Return Data to Microsoft Office Excel. Click Finish to close the wizard and to open the Import Data dialog box.
9   Specify whether you want to place the data in the existing worksheet or in a new worksheet.
10 Click OK to import the data.

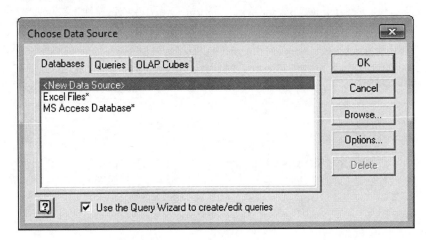

Exhibit 6-4: The Choose Data Source dialog box

Do it!   **B-1:   Getting external data from Microsoft Query**

The files for this activity are in Student Data folder **Unit 6\Topic B**.

Here's how	Here's why
1 Open Query.xlsx	(You might need to select Excel Files from the Files of type list in the Open dialog box.) This workbook contains two worksheets. QueryDb is the active sheet. You'll use the Microsoft Query program to retrieve data from an Access database and place it in this worksheet.
2 Save the workbook as **My Query.xlsx**	In the current topic folder.
3 Click the **Data** tab	
4 In the Get External Data group, click **From Other Sources**	To display a list of sources.
Choose **From Microsoft Query**	To open the Choose Data Source dialog box, as shown in Exhibit 6-4. By default, the Databases tab is active. You can either select an existing data source or create a new one.
5 Verify that **<New Data Source>** is selected	
Click **OK**	To open the Create New Data Source dialog box.
6 In the first box, enter **Employee**	What name do you want to give your data source? 1. Employee
	To specify the name of the new data source.
7 In the second box, click the arrow and select the indicated option	Driver da Microsoft para arquivos texto (*.txt; *.csv) Driver do Microsoft Access (*.mdb) Driver do Microsoft dBase (*.dbf) Driver do Microsoft Excel(*.xls) Driver do Microsoft Paradox (*.db) Driver para o Microsoft Visual FoxPro Microsoft Access Driver (*.mdb) Microsoft Access Driver (*.mdb, *.accdb) Microsoft Access Text Driver (*.txt, *.csv)
	To specify the database driver.
8 Click **Connect**	To open the ODBC Microsoft Access Setup dialog box.

9 Under Database, click **Select**

To open the Select Database dialog box.

From the Directories list, navigate to the current topic folder

(If necessary.) To specify the folder that contains the database.

From the Database Name list, select **Employee.accdb**

Database Name
Employee.accdb
Employee.accdb

To specify the database from which you'll import data.

10 Click **OK**

To return to the ODBC Microsoft Access Setup dialog box.

Click **OK**

To return to the Create New Data Source dialog box.

11 From the last list, select **Employees**

Select a default table
4. Employees
Departments
Employees
Query1
Sales employees

To specify which of the tables in the Employee database should act as the default for building queries.

12 Click **OK**

To return to the Choose Data Source dialog box. The Employee data source has been added to the list and is selected.

13 Click **OK**

To close the Choose Data Source dialog box and open the Choose Columns page of the Query Wizard. In the "Available tables and columns" list, Employees is selected.

Click [>]

Columns in your query:
Ecode
Lname
Fname
Region
Dept code

To include all columns of the Employees table in the query. The columns of the Employees table now appear in the "Columns in your query" list.

14	Click **Next**	To open the Filter Data page of the Query Wizard. The group box under "Only include rows where" is not available and has no name.
	From the Column to filter list, select **Dept code**	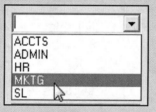
		The group box under "Only include rows where" is now available and is named "Dept code." The first list under Dept code is also available.
	From the first list under Dept code, select **equals**	To specify the comparison operator for the query.
	From the second list under Dept code, select **MKTG**	
		To specify that the result of this query includes only those rows where the Dept code is MKTG.
15	Click **Next**	To open the Sort Order page of the Query Wizard.
	From the Sort by list, select **Region**	This will sort data by Region. By default, Ascending is selected.
16	Click **Next**	To open the Finish page of the Query Wizard. By default, Return Data to Microsoft Office Excel is selected.
17	Click **Finish**	The Import Data dialog box appears, prompting you to specify the destination for the data. Cell A1 in the existing worksheet is selected by default.
18	Click **OK**	To close the dialog box and import the data. The records of all employees in the Marketing department appear in the worksheet.
19	Update the workbook	

The Web query feature

Explanation

If you want to analyze data on the Web, such as online currency rates or stock quotes, you can create a Web query. When you run a Web query, Excel retrieves data that has been marked up with Hypertext Markup Language (HTML) or Extensible Markup Language (XML).

HTML and XML

The focus of HTML, which consists primarily of predefined tags, is the appearance of the content in a browser window. XML, on the other hand, focuses on the content and not on its appearance. There are no predefined tags in XML; instead, you create your own tags to give your data meaning and structure. Both markup languages are related to a parent language, SGML (Standard Generalized Markup Language), which provides rules for marking up documents and data.

Retrieving data from the Web

To retrieve data from a Web page:

1   Click the Data tab. Then, in the Get External Data group, click From Web to open the New Web Query dialog box.
2   In the Address box, enter the address of the Web page from which you want to retrieve data, as shown in Exhibit 6-5.
3   Click the arrow next to the table you want to select.
4   Click Options to open the Web Query Options dialog box. Select the format in which you want the data to be displayed. Click OK.
5   Click Import to open the Import Data dialog box. Specify whether you want the data to be placed in an existing worksheet or a new worksheet. Click OK.

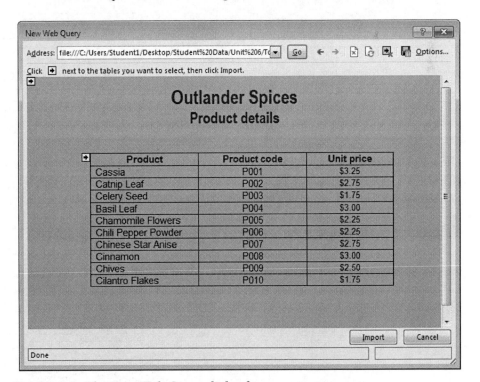

Exhibit 6-5: The New Web Query dialog box

Do it!

B-2: Using a Web query to get data from the Web

The files for this activity are in Student Data folder **Unit 6\Topic B**.

Here's how	Here's why
1 Click the WebQ sheet	You'll use the Web query program to retrieve data from a Web page.
Click the **Data** tab	If necessary.
2 In the Get External Data group, click **From Web**	To open the New Web Query dialog box.
3 In the Address box, enter **C:\Users*User name*\Desktop\ Student Data\Unit *6*\Topic *B*\Product.htm**	
	(Use the current unit number and topic letter.) This is the address of the Web page that contains the relevant data.
Click **Go**	The preview of the Web page appears in the dialog box.
4 Click the arrow to the left of the table, as shown	
	To import data from the table on the Web page.
5 Click **Options**, as shown	
	To open the Web Query Options dialog box.
Under Formatting, select **Full HTML formatting**	To retain the current formatting of the table.
Click **OK**	
6 Click **Import**	To open the Import Data dialog box. By default, the Existing worksheet option is selected.
Click **OK**	

	A	B	C
1	Product	Product code	Unit price
2	Cassia	P001	$3.25
3	Catnip Leaf	P002	$2.75
4	Celery Seed	P003	$1.75
5	Basil Leaf	P004	$3.00
6	Chamomile Flowers	P005	$2.25
7	Chili Pepper Powder	P006	$2.25
8	Chinese Star Anise	P007	$2.75
9	Cinnamon	P008	$3.00

The data from the table on the Web page appears in the worksheet.

7 Update and close the workbook

Unit summary: Exporting and importing data

Topic A In this topic, you **exported data** from Excel to a text file. You **imported data** from a text file into an Excel workbook. You also separated the imported data into columns.

Topic B In this topic, you used **Microsoft Query** to retrieve data from an Access database. You also learned how to use the **Web query** feature to retrieve data from Web pages in HTML or XML format.

Independent practice activity

In this activity, you'll export data from a worksheet to a text file, and you'll work with data using Microsoft Query.

The files for this activity are in Student Data folder **Unit 6\Unit summary**.

1 Open East sales.xlsx. (Verify that Export is the active worksheet.)

2 Export data from the Export worksheet to a text file. Save the text file as **My East sales**. (*Hint:* When prompted, export only the current sheet.)

3 Open the exported file in Notepad. (Because some product names are longer or shorter than others, the tabbed columns might not look neat.) Close Notepad.

4 Click the Importing practice worksheet. Using Microsoft Query, select or create an Employee database connection. (*Hint:* On the Data tab, click From Other Sources and choose From Microsoft Query. If Employee does not appear in the Databases panel, select <New Data Source>; then click OK and enter data source information for the Employees database.)

5 Add all of the columns of the Employees table to your query.

6 Include only those records with a Dept code value that equals SL.

7 Sort the data by the last name (Lname) field, in ascending order.

8 Place the resulting data in cell A1 of the current sheet. Check the result against Exhibit 6-6.

9 Save the workbook as **My exporting practice** in Excel workbook format.

10 Update and close the workbook.

	A	B	C	D	E
1	Ecode	Lname	Fname	Region	Dept code
2	E-02	Lee	Shannon	South	SL
3	E-03	McGregor	Melinda	West	SL
4	E-04	Overmire	James	North	SL
5	E-01	Pingault	Malcolm	East	SL

Exhibit 6-6: The worksheet as it appears after Step 8

Review questions

1 True or false? An Excel workbook that's saved in a different file format will retain its original formatting.

2 When exporting Excel data to a text format, row data will be separated by

   A Commas.

   B Paragraph marks.

   C Tabs.

   D Spaces.

3 Which of the following file types will preserve all the formatting of an Excel workbook? (Choose all that apply.)

   A XML Paper Specification (XPS).

   B Portable Document Format (PDF).

   C Text (tab delimited).

   D Open Document Spreadsheet (ODS).

4 Which Excel feature will help you easily divide text fields into two or more columns?.

5 What is Microsoft Query?

Unit 7
Analytical tools

Complete this unit, and you'll know how to:

A Use the Goal Seek utility to meet a target output for a formula by changing the values in the input cells.

B Create scenarios to save various sets of input values that produce different results.

Topic A: Goal Seek

What-if analysis

Explanation

You might want a formula to return a specific result, but you might not know the input values that will provide that result. For example, you might want to take out a loan for which the maximum monthly payment is $500. Based on this, you might want to know a possible combination of period, interest rate, and principal amount. In this case, you can use the Goal Seek utility to find the input values.

You can use the Goal Seek utility to perform a *what-if analysis*. This type of analysis involves changing the values in a worksheet and observing how these changes affect the results of the formulas. You use Goal Seek to solve problems that have one variable.

The Goal Seek utility

Use the Goal Seek utility to solve a formula based on the value that you want the formula to return. To use the Goal Seek utility:

1 Click the Data tab.
2 In the Data Tools group, click What-If Analysis and choose Goal Seek to open the Goal Seek dialog box.
3 In the Set cell box, specify the cell that contains the formula you want to solve.
4 In the To value box, enter the result you want.
5 In the By changing cell box, specify the cell that contains the value you want to adjust.
6 Click OK.

Do it!

A-1:   Using Goal Seek to solve for a single variable

The files for this activity are in Student Data folder **Unit 7\Topic A**.

Here's how	Here's why
1 Open Loan analysis.xlsx	
Save the workbook as **My Loan analysis.xlsx**	In the current topic folder.
2 Select E6	This cell displays a monthly payment of -$3,417.76 for a loan amount of $100,000. You'll use Goal Seek to calculate the loan amount that you can obtain if you can afford a monthly payment of $10,000, given a period of 36 months and an interest rate of 14%.
Observe the formula bar	=PMT(D6%/12,C6,B6)
	The PMT function calculates the monthly payment for the loan amount in B6 based on the annual interest rate in D6 and the repayment period in C6.

3   Click the **Data** tab

In the Data Tools group, click **What-If Analysis**

Choose **Goal Seek...**

To open the What-If Analysis menu.

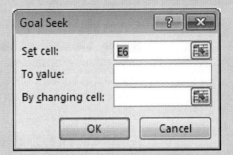

To open the Goal Seek dialog box. The Set cell box contains E6. This cell contains the formula you want to solve.

4   In the To value box, enter **-10000**

This is the result you want the formula in E6 to return.

In the "By changing cell" box, enter **B6**

This is the cell containing the loan amount: the value that will be adjusted.

5   Click **OK**

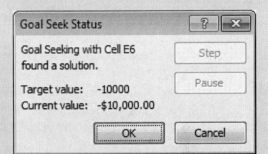

The Goal Seek Status dialog box opens. It states that Goal Seek has found a solution, which you can accept or reject. The target value is the value you asked the formula to return. The current value is the solution found by Goal Seek.

6   Click **OK**

To close the dialog box.

Observe the value in B6

With a monthly payment of $10,000, a period of 36 months, and an interest rate of 14%, you can afford a loan of $292,589.

7   Find the loan amount that you can obtain from the NewCiti bank if you pay $15,000 per month for 42 months

(Use Goal Seek.) You'll get $487,820 as the loan amount.

8   Update and close the workbook

Topic B: Scenarios

Creating a scenario

Explanation

Scenarios are sets of input values that produce different results. For example, in a budget projection worksheet, you can have one scenario that includes conservative sales figures, and another scenario that includes more aggressive sales figures. Instead of creating new scenarios every time, you can modify existing scenarios. In a worksheet containing multiple scenarios, you can switch among them to view the results for different input values. In addition, you can merge scenarios from other worksheets.

You can use the Scenario Manager dialog box to create a scenario. Here's how:

1   Click the Data tab.
2   From the What-If Analysis menu in the Data Tools group, choose Scenario Manager to open the Scenario Manager dialog box.
3   Click the Add button to open the Add Scenario dialog box.
4   In the Scenario name box, enter a name for the scenario.
5   In the Changing cells box, specify the cells that contain the values you want to change. Click OK.
6   In the Scenario Values dialog box, specify values for the changing cells, and click OK.

After creating the scenario, you can modify it by editing values for the changing cells. To edit values:

1   Open the Scenario Manager dialog box and select the scenario you want to change.
2   Click Edit to open the Edit Scenario dialog box.
3   Click OK to open the Scenario Values dialog box.
4   Specify values for the changing cells and click OK.

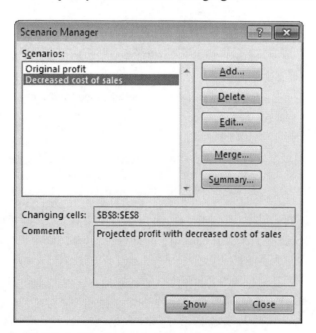

Exhibit 7-1: The Scenario Manager dialog box

Do it!

B-1:   Creating scenarios

The files for this activity are in Student Data folder **Unit 7\Topic B**.

Here's how	Here's why
1 Open Projections.xlsx	
Save the workbook as **My Projections.xlsx**	In the current topic folder.
2 Click the Scenarios sheet	(If necessary.) You'll create scenarios to see how different Cost-of-sales values will affect the Gross profit, Net profit, and Profit %.
3 Select B8:E8	The cost of sales for the four quarters.
Click the **Data** tab	If necessary.
From the What-If Analysis menu, choose **Scenario Manager...**	To open the Scenario Manager dialog box. Currently, no scenarios are defined.
Click **Add**	To open the Add Scenario dialog box.
4 In the Scenario name box, enter **Original profit**	This is the name of the scenario that will preserve the original values. The Changing cells box displays the references of the selected cells.
Edit the Comment box to read **Original projected profit**	To describe the scenario.
Click **OK**	 **Scenario Values** Enter values for each of the changing cells. 1: $B$8 25000 2: $C$8 42050 3: $D$8 59450 4: $E$8 60450 To open the Scenario Values dialog box. The current values of the selected cells are displayed.
5 Click **Add**	To add the Original profit scenario to the Scenarios list and return to the Add Scenario dialog box. This scenario will preserve the original values in changing cells.
6 In the Scenario name box, enter **Decreased cost of sales**	This is the name of the scenario you are about to create.
Edit the Comment box to read **Projected profit with decreased cost of sales**	To describe the new scenario.
Click **OK**	To open the Scenario Values dialog box.

7	Enter the values as shown	**Scenario Values** Enter values for each of the changing cells. 1: $B$8 23000 2: $C$8 40000 3: $D$8 55000 4: $E$8 55000
8	Click **OK**	To return to the Scenario Manager dialog box, shown in Exhibit 7-1. The Scenarios list displays the names of the two scenarios you just defined.
9	Click **Show**	To apply the "Decreased cost of sales" scenario. The values in the range B8:E8 change according to the values stored in this scenario. Based on the new Cost-of-sales values, the values for Gross profit, Net profit, and Profit % also change. You'll edit the scenario to lower the Cost-of-sales values even more.
10	Click **Edit**	To open the Edit Scenario dialog box. The Scenario name box contains "Decreased cost of sales."
	Click **OK**	To open the Scenario Values dialog box. All of the boxes display the current values of the selected cells.
11	Type the values shown	**Scenario Values** Enter values for each of the changing cells. 1: $B$8 20000 2: $C$8 35000 3: $D$8 50000 4: $E$8 48000
	Click **OK**	To return to the Scenario Manager dialog box.
	Click **Show**	To apply the changes made in the scenario.
	Click **Close**	The values for Cost of sales, Gross profit, Net profit, and Profit % have changed.
12	Update the workbook	

Switching among scenarios

Explanation

You can switch among scenarios to view results based on different input values. To display a scenario, open the Scenario Manager dialog box, select the name of the scenario you want to display, and click the Show button.

If you have a worksheet with many scenarios, you can switch among them more easily by adding the Scenario list to the Quick Access toolbar. To add buttons to the Quick Access toolbar:

1 On the Quick Access toolbar, click Customize Quick Access Toolbar and choose More Commands. The Excel Options dialog box opens with the Quick Access Toolbar settings displayed.

2 From the Available commands list, select the category that contains the command you want to add, or select All Commands. Some commands are available only in the list of all commands.

3 Select the command you want to add to the toolbar and click Add.

4 If desired, click Move Up or Move Down to change the command's position relative to the other commands on the toolbar.

5 Click OK to close the Excel Options dialog box.

Do it!

B-2: Switching among scenarios

Here's how	Here's why
1 Observe F15	The Profit % is 36.
2 On the Quick Access toolbar, click as shown	 To display the Customize Quick Access Toolbar menu.
Choose **More Commands...**	To open the Excel Options dialog box, with the Quick Access Toolbar page active.
3 From the "Choose commands from" list, select **Data tab**	The Scenario Manager is on the Data tab.
4 In the list of commands, select **Scenario Manager...**	The commands are listed in alphabetical order.
In the Customize Quick Access Toolbar list, verify that **For all documents (default)** is selected	To ensure that the button you'll add is available in all documents, not just the active one.
5 Click **Add**	To add the command to the Quick Access toolbar.
6 From the "Choose commands from" list, select **All commands**	

7 In the list of commands, select
Scenario

   Click **Add** | To add the command to the Quick Access toolbar.

8 Click **OK** | To close the Excel Options dialog box.

9 On the Quick Access toolbar, click as shown

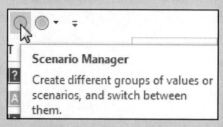

To open the Scenario Manager dialog box.

   Select **Original profit**

   Click **Show** | To display the Original profit scenario. This scenario will now be added to the Scenario button you added earlier.

   Click **Close**

10 On the Quick Access toolbar, click as shown

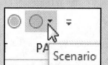

To display the Scenario list.

   Select **Decreased cost of sales** | You can use this list to switch among scenarios.

11 Update the workbook

Merging scenarios

Explanation

You can merge scenarios from different worksheets so that all scenarios in a source worksheet are copied to the active worksheet. The changing cells in the active worksheet correspond to those in the source worksheet. This ensures that the changes made in the source worksheet are reflected in the active worksheet.

To merge scenarios:

1   Click the worksheet where you want to merge scenarios.
2   Open the Scenario Manager dialog box.
3   Click Merge.
4   From the Sheet list, select the worksheet that contains the scenarios you want to merge.
5   Click OK.

The Scenario Summary report

A Scenario Summary report displays the original and current values for the changing cells corresponding to available scenarios. To create a Scenario Summary report:

1   Open the Scenario Manager dialog box.
2   Click Summary to open the Scenario Summary dialog box.
3   In the Result cells box, select the cells that contain the values changed by scenarios.
4   Click OK.

Scenario Summary			
	Current Values:	Original profit	Decreased cost of sales
Changing Cells:			
$B$8	20000	25000	20000
$C$8	35000	42050	35000
$D$8	50000	59450	50000
$E$8	48000	60450	48000
Result Cells:			
$E$8	48000	60450	48000
$C$9	43200	36150	43200
Notes: Current Values column represents values of changing cells at time Scenario Summary Report was created. Changing cells for each scenario are highlighted in gray.			

Exhibit 7-2: A sample Scenario Summary

Do it!   **B-3:   Merging scenarios from another worksheet**

Here's how	Here's why
1 Click the Scenarios 2 sheet	You'll merge scenarios to this worksheet from the Scenarios worksheet.
Observe F15	The Profit % is 25.
2 Open the Scenario Manager dialog box	(Click the Scenario Manager button on the Quick Access toolbar.) There are no scenarios in the Scenarios 2 worksheet.
3 Click **Merge**	Merge Scenarios Merge scenarios from Book: My Projections.xlsx Sheet: Scenarios Scenarios 2 There are 2 scenarios on source sheet. To open the Merge Scenarios dialog box. The Book box displays the name of the workbook from which you'll merge scenarios. The Sheet list contains the worksheets in the workbook.
Verify that **Scenarios** is selected	You'll merge the scenarios in this worksheet.
4 Click **OK**	To return to the Scenario Manager dialog box. The Scenarios list displays the names of the two scenarios you just merged. By default, Original profit is selected.
5 Select **Decreased cost of sales** and click **Show**	To apply the "Decreased cost of sales" scenario. The values for Cost of sales, Gross profit, Net profit, and Profit % change according to the values stored in the scenario.
Observe F15	The Profit % has increased to 36% in the Scenarios 2 worksheet.

6 Click **Summary**

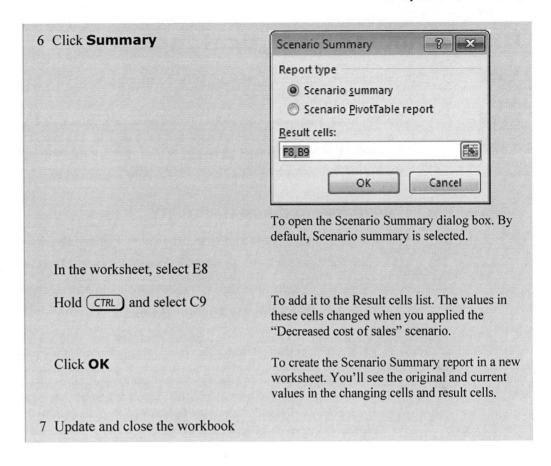

To open the Scenario Summary dialog box. By default, Scenario summary is selected.

In the worksheet, select E8

Hold ⟨ CTRL ⟩ and select C9

To add it to the Result cells list. The values in these cells changed when you applied the "Decreased cost of sales" scenario.

Click **OK**

To create the Scenario Summary report in a new worksheet. You'll see the original and current values in the changing cells and result cells.

7 Update and close the workbook

Unit summary: Analytical tools

Topic A   In this topic, you used **Goal Seek** to find a specific result for a formula by changing the value of one of the input cells.

Topic B   In this topic, you created and edited **scenarios**. You learned that scenarios are used to save sets of input values that produce different results. Then, you switched among scenarios to view different data results in a worksheet. In addition, you merged scenarios and created a Scenario Summary report.

Independent practice activity

In this activity, you'll use Goal Seek to calculate values. You'll also create scenarios.

The files for this activity are in Student Data folder **Unit 7\Unit summary**.

1 Open Analysis practice.xlsx. Goal seeking should be the active worksheet.

2 Save the workbook as **My Analysis practice.xlsx**.

3 In D6, use Goal Seek to calculate the loan amount in C6 for a monthly deduction of **$2,300**. (*Hint:* Cell C6 is the cell to be changed. The loan amount will be $108,250.)

4 Click the Scenarios worksheet. Create a scenario for the current cost of sales in the worksheet. Name it **Current profit**. Then, create a second scenario called **Projected profit**, and change the values in B8:E8 to **21000**, **41500**, **54700**, and **58000**, respectively. The total profit should change from 25% to 29%.

5 Update and close the workbook.

Review questions

1 Describe a what-if analysis.

2 True or false? Goal Seek is used when you want to solve a problem with more than one variable.

3 What is a scenario?

4 List the steps you would use to change a scenario.

5 Describe how you can switch between scenarios.

Unit 8

Macros and Visual Basic

Complete this unit, and you'll know how to:

A Create and run macros to automate complex and repetitive tasks.

B Use the Visual Basic Editor to edit a macro.

Topic A: Running and recording a macro

Running macros

Explanation

You can use macros to automate complex and repetitive tasks. A *macro* is a series of instructions that execute automatically with a single command. For example, you can create a macro to format a worksheet or to print a report. You can use the macros already available in Excel or create your own. To make macros more convenient to use, you can assign them to Quick Access toolbar buttons.

To run macros in a workbook, you first need to display the Developer tab on the ribbon. To do so, open the Excel Options dialog box, and click Customize Ribbon. Under Customize the Ribbon, in the Main Tabs list, check Developer. Then click OK.

To run a macro, click the Developer tab. In the Code group, click Macros to open the Macro dialog box, shown in Exhibit 8-1. Select the desired macro and click Run.

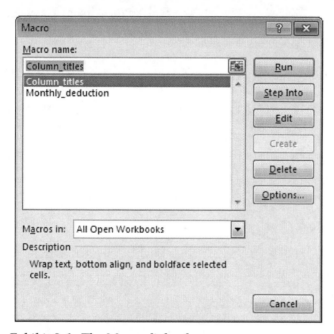

Exhibit 8-1: The Macro dialog box

Enabling macros

Macros can contain viruses that can harm your computer. To combat this problem, Excel requires you to enable macros after opening a file that contains them. To enable macros, click Enable Content in the Security Warning bar that appears.

If Windows is set to display file-name extensions, you can use them to distinguish an Excel file that contains macros from an Excel file without macros. A standard Excel 2013 file uses the extension .xlsx; an Excel 2013 file with macro code uses the extension .xlsm.

Trust Center macro settings

You can protect your computer from potentially dangerous macros by using one of the following macro settings in the Trust Center:

- Disable all macros without notification
- Disable all macros with notification (default setting)
- Disable all macros except digitally signed macros
- Enable all macros (not recommended)

To change the default setting, click Macro Security in the Code group on the Developer tab. The Trust Center dialog box opens, with Macro Settings selected in the left pane. Select the desired macro security setting and click OK.

Do it!

A-1: Running a macro

The files for this activity are in Student Data folder **Unit 8\Topic A**.

Here's how	Here's why
1 Open Running macros.xlsm	This document contains macros, which are disabled by default. You'll enable the macros so you can run them.
2 In the Security Warning bar that appears, click **Enable Content**	

> ⚠ SECURITY WARNING   Macros have been disabled.   [Enable Content]

	(Above the formula bar.) To enable the macros included in the workbook.
3 Open the Save As dialog box	
In the File name box, enter **My macros**	
Observe that Excel Macro-Enabled Workbook is selected in the Save as type list	Excel 2013 files with macros are saved as a different file type, with the extension .xlsm instead of .xlsx.
Click **Save**	To save the file in the current topic folder.

4 Open the Excel Options dialog box	(Click the File tab.) You need to display the Developer tab on the ribbon in order to work with macros.
Click **Customize Ribbon**	
Under Customize the Ribbon, in the Main Tabs list, check **Developer**	
Click **OK**	To close Excel Options and return to the worksheet. The Developer tab is now on the ribbon.
5 Select A4:D4	You'll run the Column_titles macro to wrap the text in the selected cells.
On the Developer tab, in the Code group, click **Macros**	To open the Macro dialog box. It lists the names of available macros, as shown in Exhibit 8-1.
Observe that the Column_titles macro is selected	
Click **Run**	To run the macro. Notice that the text in the cells is wrapped to multiple lines as necessary, bottom-aligned, and bold.
6 Select E4	The macros in this workbook were assigned shortcut keys. You'll use one to run the Column_titles macro.
Press CTRL + SHIFT + C	The text is formatted to match the other column titles.
7 Select E5	The cell for Michael Lee's monthly deduction amount.
Run the Monthly_deduction macro	(Use the Macro dialog box.) The monthly deduction amount appears in E5.
8 Select E5	=PMT(10%/12,D5,-C5)
	The formula for the PMT function appears in the formula bar. This formula was entered by the macro you just ran.
9 Select E6	
Press CTRL + SHIFT + M	To run the Monthly_deduction macro using its assigned shortcut key.
10 Update and close the workbook	

Recording macros

Explanation

To create a macro, you can write the Visual Basic code for it, or you can have Excel record actions as you perform them. Recording is simpler, but creates more lines of code; this can be less efficient if you want to edit the macro later.

To record a macro:

1   In the status bar, click the Record Macro button to open the Record Macro dialog box.

2   Specify a macro name and a shortcut key. Macro names can include letters, numbers, and underscores. Names must begin with a letter and cannot contain spaces.

3   Click OK to start recording the macro.

4   Perform the actions you want to include in the macro. As you work, Excel records the sequence of steps.

5   When you're finished, click the Stop Recording button in the status bar.

Exhibit 8-2: The Column_titles macro in the Record Macro dialog box

Saving files with macros

When you add a macro to a file that didn't contain any and you then save the file, Excel displays a message box, warning you that it will save the file without macros. The default Yes response will delete any macros you've recorded. Click No to stop saving; then choose File, Save As and save the file in the Excel Macro-Enabled Workbook format.

Do it!

A-2:   Recording a macro

The files for this activity are in Student Data folder **Unit 8\Topic A**.

Here's how	Here's why
1 Open Loan details.xlsx	You'll record a macro to format column titles.
2 Save the workbook as **My Loan details.xlsx**	
3 Select E4	This cell should be formatted as a column heading. When you want a macro to be associated with a particular cell, select that cell before turning on the recorder.
In the status bar, click 📇	To open the Record Macro dialog box.
4 Edit the Macro name box to read **Column_titles**	
Click in the Shortcut key box	
Press (SHIFT) + (C)	Shortcut key: Ctrl+Shift+ d
	To define the shortcut key for the Column_titles macro as Ctrl+Shift+C. (Excel adds the Ctrl part.)
In the "Store macro in" list, verify that **This Workbook** is selected	To specify that the macro will be stored in only the active workbook. This means it will not be available in other workbooks.
In the Description box, enter **Wrap text, bottom align, and bold selected cells.**	As shown in Exhibit 8-2.
5 Click **OK**	The Stop Recording button appears in the status bar.
6 Click the **Home** tab	If necessary.
In the Alignment group, click ▤	To make the text wrap to multiple lines.
Click ▤	To left-align the text in the cell.
Click ▤	To position the text at the bottom of the cell.
In the Font group, click B	To apply bold formatting. You've completed all of the steps you want the macro to perform.

7 In the status bar, click 	To stop recording.
8 Save the workbook as **My recorded macros**	A message box appears, warning you that you can't save a file with a macro in a standard workbook file.
Click **No**	The Save As dialog box opens.
9 From the Save as type list, select **Excel Macro-Enabled Workbook (*.xlsm)**	To save the file as a workbook with code.
Click **Save**	To save the workbook and close the dialog box.
10 Select A4	(If necessary.) You'll test the macro you recorded.
Run the Column_titles macro	(Press Ctrl+Shift+C.) The title is formatted as you specified.
11 Update the workbook	

Inserting macro buttons in the worksheet

Explanation

To run a macro by clicking a button in the worksheet, you need to assign a macro to the specific button or shape object. You can either insert a new button and assign a macro to it, or assign a macro to an existing object.

To assign a macro to an existing object, right-click the object and choose Assign Macro. Then select the macro and click OK.

To insert a button (a form control) and assign a macro to it, use the following steps:

1 On the Developer tab, in the Controls group, click Insert.
2 From the Controls gallery, shown in Exhibit 8-3, select Button (Form Control).
3 Drag to draw the button in the worksheet. When you release the mouse, the Assign Macro dialog box appears.
4 Select the macro you want to run when the button is clicked.
5 Click OK.

Exhibit 8-3: The Controls gallery

Modifying the button (form control) properties

Once the button has been inserted, you can edit the button text and change its appearance, as with any other Excel object. To select the button without running the assigned macro, right-click the button.

From the shortcut menu, you can do the following:

- Choose Edit Text to change the button text.
- Choose Assign Macro to change the assigned macro.
- Choose Format Control to open the Format Control dialog box, shown in Exhibit 8-4. Use the Font, Alignment, Size, Protection, Properties, Margins, and Alt Text tabs to format the button.

Exhibit 8-4: The Format Control dialog box

Do it!   **A-3:   Inserting a macro button**

Here's how	Here's why
1 On the Developer tab, in the Controls group, click **Insert**	To display a gallery of controls.
2 Click **Button (Form Control)**, as shown	

Form Controls

Button (Form Control)

	The mouse pointer changes to a crosshair.
3 In an empty area of the worksheet, drag to draw a button	The exact size is not important.
Release the mouse pointer	The Assign Macro dialog box appears.
4 From the Macro Name list, select **Column_titles**	To assign this macro to the newly drawn button.
Click **OK**	To close the Assign Macro dialog box. "Button 1" appears on the new button.
5 Right-click the button and choose **Edit Text**	You'll change the button text to be more descriptive.
Enter **Format Column Titles**	

Format Column Titles

	If the button is too small, drag the lower-right corner handle to increase the size of the button and display the button text.
Click the worksheet	To deselect the button.
6 Right-click the button and choose **Format Control...**	You can use the settings on these seven tabs to control the appearance of the button.
Click **Cancel**	
7 Select D4	
Click the **Format Column Titles** button	To format the column title "No. of monthly payments" in D4.
8 Update and close the workbook	

Topic B: Working with VBA code

Explanation

Excel saves the steps in a macro as Visual Basic for Applications (VBA) code. You can view and edit the code for a macro with the Visual Basic Editor.

Examining VBA code

VBA code is stored in special sheets called *modules*. A module might contain one or more sub procedures. A *sub procedure* is a named block of lines of code which, when executed, perform a sequence of steps.

VBA code consists of statements and comments. *Statements* are instructions that perform certain actions. *Comments* are non-executable lines of text used to describe sections of macro code. Comments begin with an apostrophe.

The following table describes the components of a statement:

Item	Description
Keywords	Special VBA terms that, by default, appear in blue. For example, the `Sub` keyword marks the beginning of a sub procedure, and the `End Sub` keyword marks the end of a sub procedure.
Variables	Used to store values. For example, you can use variables to store the results of a formula.
Operators	Used just as they are in a worksheet. Operators can be arithmetic (+, -, /, *) or comparison (=, >, <).
Procedure call	A statement that calls a procedure from another procedure. You can do this by inserting the name of the procedure you're calling into the procedure you are calling it from.

Observing a VBA code module

To observe a VBA code module, open the Macro dialog box. Then click the Edit button to open the Microsoft Visual Basic window. To close the code window, choose File, Close and Return to Microsoft Excel.

Do it!

B-1: Observing a VBA code module

The files for this activity are in Student Data folder **Unit 8\Topic B**.

Here's how	Here's why
1 Open Outlander Spices.xlsm	
Click **Enable Content**	To enable the macros contained in this workbook.
Save the macro-enabled workbook as **My Outlander Spices.xlsm**	In the current topic folder.

2 Open the Macro dialog box

(On the Developer tab, in the Code group, click Macros.) By default, Column_titles is selected in the Macro name list.

Click **Edit**

To open the Microsoft Visual Basic window. The workbook's name appears in the title bar.

Observe the Code window

This window displays the code for the Column_titles macro.

3 Observe the first line in the Code window

```
Sub Column_titles()
```

The Sub keyword marks the beginning of the macro. Keywords are shown in blue.

Observe the last line in the Code window

```
End Sub
```

The End Sub keyword marks the end of the macro.

4 Observe the comments

```
' Column_titles Macro
' Wrap text, bottom align, and boldface selected cells.
'
' Keyboard Shortcut: Ctrl+Shift+C
```

Comments begin with an apostrophe and describe the macro. By default, comments are green.

5 Observe the statements

Statements appear in black and instruct Excel to perform a sequence of actions. The statements are located between the Sub and End Sub keywords.

Observe the indented statement lines between the first set of With Selection and End With lines

Each group of lines between the With Selection and End With statements applies to the selected cells. Sophisticated macros can select cells other than the ones originally selected when the macro was created.

Observe the repeats of the With Selection/End With blocks

Each time you clicked a button in the Alignment group, the macro recorded all of the alignment settings. This isn't an efficient use of code because many of the lines are repeated.

Editing VBA code

Explanation

Sometimes you might need to edit the code for a macro. For example, say you have a macro that calculates the monthly deduction at an interest rate of 12%, and you want to change the interest rate to 11%. Instead of recording a new macro, you can edit the VBA code of the existing macro.

You can edit macro code in the Visual Basic Editor. Make sure you save the macro after you've made any necessary changes.

Do it!

B-2: Editing VBA code

Here's how	Here's why
1 In the three `With Selection` blocks of code, compare the `.WrapText`, `.HorizontalAlignment`, and `.VerticalAlignment` lines	Excel created each block of code when you clicked a button in the Alignment group. The first block set the `.WrapText` value to `True`, the second block set the `.HorizontalAlignment` value to `xlLeft`, and the third block set the `.VerticalAlignment` setting to `xlBottom`. Because the third block contains the settings you chose for the first two, the first two are redundant. You'll delete them to make the code more efficient.

2 Select from the first instance of `With Selection` through the second instance of `End With`, as shown	<pre>' Keyboard Shortcut: Ctrl+Shift+C
	'
	    With Selection
	        .HorizontalAlignment = xlRight
	        .VerticalAlignment = xlTop
	        .WrapText = True
	        .Orientation = 0
	        .AddIndent = False
	        .IndentLevel = 0
	        .ShrinkToFit = False
	        .ReadingOrder = xlContext
	        .MergeCells = False
	    End With
	    With Selection
	        .HorizontalAlignment = xlLeft
	        .VerticalAlignment = xlTop
	        .WrapText = True
	        .Orientation = 0
	        .AddIndent = False
	        .IndentLevel = 0
	        .ShrinkToFit = False
	        .ReadingOrder = xlContext
	        .MergeCells = False
	    End With
	    With Selection
	        .HorizontalAlignment = xlLeft</pre>
	These blocks of code are no longer necessary.

3 Press `DELETE`   To delete the selected code.

You've decided that you don't want the macro to change the horizontal alignment, so you'll delete that code as well.

4 Delete the following line:

`.HorizontalAlignment = xlLeft`

Compare your code with the code shown below

```
Sub Column_titles()
'
' Column_titles Macro
' Wrap text, bottom align, and boldface selected cells.
'
' Keyboard Shortcut: Ctrl+Shift+C
'

    With Selection
        |
        .VerticalAlignment = xlBottom
        .WrapText = True
        .Orientation = 0
        .AddIndent = False
        .IndentLevel = 0
        .ShrinkToFit = False
        .ReadingOrder = xlContext
        .MergeCells = False
    End With
    Selection.Font.Bold = True
End Sub
```

5 Click 🖫   To update the code.

Choose **File**, **Close and**   To close the Microsoft Visual Basic window.
Return to Microsoft Excel

6 Update and close the workbook

Unit summary: Macros and Visual Basic

Topic A

In this topic, you recorded and ran a **macro**. You learned that macros perform tasks automatically and can be created to meet your specific needs. Then you assigned a macro to a **command button** as well as to a button inserted into the worksheet. You also added a macro button to the Quick Access toolbar and to the ribbon. You created an **Auto_Open** macro that runs when the workbook is opened.

Topic B

In this topic, you learned that macros are saved as **VBA code**, and you examined some VBA code. Then you edited the code for a macro.

Independent practice activity

In this activity, you'll record, edit, and run several macros.

The files for this activity are in Student Data folder **Unit 8\Unit summary**.

1 Open Outlander profit.xlsx. (*Hint:* The Macros worksheet contains two scenarios: Original and Lower cost of sales. To access these scenarios, you'll click the Data tab.)

2 Save the workbook as **My Outlander profit** in the Excel Macro-Enabled Workbook file format.

3 Record a macro named **Display_lower_cost_of_sales** that has Ctrl+Shift+C as its shortcut key. This macro should show the "Lower cost of sales" scenario.

   To do this, start recording the macro. Click the Data tab, click What-If Analysis, and choose Scenario Manager. In the Scenarios list, select **Lower cost of sales**, and then click **Show**. Click **Close**; then stop recording the macro.

4 Record a macro named **Display_original** that has Ctrl+Shift+O as its shortcut key. This macro should show the Original scenario.

5 Run the Display_lower_cost_of_sales macro. Run the Display_original macro.

6 Change the name of the "Lower cost of sales" scenario to **Decreased cost of sales**. (*Hint:* Open the Scenario Manager dialog box, select **Lower cost of sales** from the Scenarios list, and click **Edit**. Do not change any other values.)

7 Edit the VBA code for the Display_lower_cost_of_sales macro to show the "Decreased cost of sales" scenario. (*Hint:* Edit the macro by replacing the argument of the ActiveSheet.Scenarios function with **Decreased cost of sales**.) Compare your VBA code window to Exhibit 8-5.

8 Update the VBA code and close the Microsoft Visual Basic window.

9 Run the edited macro.

10 Update the workbook and close it.

11 Close Excel.

```
Sub Display_lower_cost_of_sales()
'
' Display_lower_cost_of_sales Macro
' Display the lower cost of sales scenario
'
' Keyboard Shortcut: Ctrl+Shift+C
'
    ActiveSheet.Scenarios("Decreased cost of sales").Show
End Sub
Sub Display_original()
'
' Display_original Macro
' Display original scenario
'
' Keyboard Shortcut: Ctrl+Shift+O
'
    ActiveSheet.Scenarios("Original").Show
End Sub
```

Exhibit 8-5: The edited VBA code for the Display_lower_cost_of_sales macro

Review questions

1 What is a macro?

2 Describe how you would change the macro security settings.

3 List two ways to create a macro.

4 In what type of code, or language, does Excel save macros? Where can you view and edit this code?

5 Where is VBA code stored?

6 True or false? A comment is an executable line of VBA code.

Course summary

This summary contains information to help you bring the course to a successful conclusion. Using this information, you will be able to:

A Use the summary text to reinforce what you've learned in class.

B Determine the other resources that might help you continue to learn about Excel 2013.

Topic A: Course summary

Use the following summary text to reinforce what you've learned in class.

Unit summaries

Unit 1

In this unit, you used the **logical functions** IF, and IFERROR to evaluate a condition and return a value based on whether that condition is true or false. Next, you used the **math** and **statistical functions** SUMIF, SUMIFS, COUNTIF, COUNTIFS, AVERAGEIF, and AVERAGEIFS to conditionally summarize, count, and average data. You used the **PMT function** to calculate the periodic payment for a loan. Then, they used text functions to separate data strings. They used **date functions** to calculate the difference between two dates. Finally, they created an **array formula** that performed multiple calculations on multiple sets to obtain multiple results, and created an array formula using a SUM function.

Unit 2

In this unit, you used the **VLOOKUP** and **HLOOKUP** functions to find a specific value in a worksheet. They used the **MATCH** function to find the relative position of a value in a range. They also used the **INDEX** function to find a value in a range by specifying a row number and column number. Finally, you created one-variable and two-variable **data tables** to project values.

Unit 3

In this unit, you created **data validation** rules to control data entered in cells. Next, they used the **Custom AutoFilter** dialog box to specify multiple conditions, using comparison criteria and comparison operators. Then, you created a **criteria range** to specify complex search conditions based on multiple column headings, and **copied filtered data** to a new location.

Unit 4

In this unit, you adjusted the scale of a **chart**. They formatted **data points** and exploded slices in a pie chart to highlight data. Then, they created a combination chart by using two value axes. You also added a **trendline** to a chart and inserted **sparklines** in a worksheet. They also created a **custom chart template**. Then, you added, formatted, and moved **drawing objects** and shapes in a chart.

Unit 5

In this unit, you created a **PivotTable**. They added fields, changed views, and created **slicers** for the PivotTable. Then, you formatted PivotTable data by applying a style and changing field settings. Finally, they created **PivotCharts** to graphically display the PivotTable data.

Unit 6

In this unit, you learned how to **export data** from Excel to other formats. You also **imported data** from a text file. Finally, they used **Microsoft Query** to retrieve data from an Access database, and they used the **Web query** feature to get data from a Web page.

Unit 7

In this unit, you used **Goal Seek** to meet a target output for a formula by adjusting the values in the input cells. Next, you created **scenarios** to save various sets of values in a worksheet.

Unit 8

In this unit, you ran a **macro** that automatically performed tasks. You recorded a macro and assigned the macro to a button inserted into the worksheet. Next, they **edited** the VBA code for a macro.

Topic B: Continued learning after class

It is impossible to learn how to use any software effectively in a single day. To get the most out of this class, you should begin working with Excel 2013 to perform real tasks as soon as possible. We also offer resources for continued learning.

Next courses in this series

This is the last course in this series.

Other resources

For more information on this and other topics, go to **www.Crisp360.com**.

Crisp360 is an online community where you can expand your knowledge base, connect with other professionals, and purchase individual training solutions.

Glossary

Array

A collection of rows or columns that is usually defined as a cell address. However, arrays can also be defined as raw data or values, otherwise known as *array constants*.

Array formula

A formula that performs multiple calculations on one or more sets of values, and then returns either a single result or multiple results. You must press Ctrl+Shift+Enter to create an array formula, which is enclosed in braces { }.

Arguments

The values that a function uses for calculations.

Circular reference

An error created when a formula refers to the cell containing the formula.

Comments

Non-executable lines of text used to describe sections of macro code.

Data table

A range that displays the results of changing certain values in one or more formulas.

Date functions

Functions used to insert the dates or to calculate length of time in terms of years, months, or days.

Field

A category of data in a PivotTable.

Goal Seek utility

A tool used to solve a formula based on the value that you want the formula to return.

HLOOKUP

A horizontal lookup function used to find values in a table that has column labels.

Input cell

The location where various values are substituted from a data table.

Iteration

The repeated recalculation of worksheet formulas until the maximum number of calculations is reached.

Leader line

A line used in a chart to connect a data label to its associated data point.

Macro

A series of instructions that are executed automatically with a single command.

Microsoft Query

A program used to retrieve data that meets certain conditions in one or more tables of a database.

Modules

The special sheets in which VBA code is stored.

Nested function

A function that serves as an argument of another function.

ODS (Open Document Spreadsheet)

A file format that maintains some formatting, but not all, when Excel data is exported to it. ODS files can be opened in other spreadsheet applications, such as Google Docs.

OLAP (Online Analytical Processing)

A type of database that stores data to be analyzed. In an OLAP database, the relationships and hierarchies are stored in OLAP cubes, which provide a multi-dimensional way to look at data.

PDF (Portable Document Format)

A file format that preserves formatting and enables file sharing. PDF provides a standard format for use by commercial printers. Adobe Reader is available as a free download.

PivotChart

A chart created from PivotTable data. The row fields of the PivotTable become the categories, and the column fields become the series. Click the field buttons in the PivotChart to change what the chart displays.

PivotTable

An interactive table that summarizes, organizes, and compares large amounts of data in a worksheet. You can rotate the rows and columns in a PivotTable to obtain different views of the same data.

Quick Style buttons

Buttons located on the Format tab and used to apply several formatting properties at once to a selected graphic.

Record

A row of data in a database.

Scenario

A set of input values that produce different results.

Slicer

A PivotTable feature that is used to filter data.

Source data

The data on which a PivotTable is based.

Sparkline

A small chart that is inserted into a single cell to illustrate a pattern or trend in data.

Sub procedure

A procedure containing the code which, when executed, performs a sequence of steps.

Trendline

A graphical representation of drifts or variations in a data series.

VBA (Visual Basic for Applications)

The code, or language, in which Excel saves the steps of a macro.

VLOOKUP

A vertical lookup function used to find values in a table that has row labels.

What-if analysis

The process of changing the values in a worksheet and observing how these changes affect the results of formulas.

XML (Extensible Markup Language)

A set of rules for structuring and designing data formats that are exchanged between applications.

XPS (XML Paper Specification

A file format that preserves formatting and graphics when Excel data is exported to it. XPS Viewer is installed by default.

Index